Strictly Come Dancing

2018
ANNUAL

In loving memory of Sir Bruce Forsyth, 1928–2017

Strictly Come Dancing

2018

ANNUAL

CONTENTS

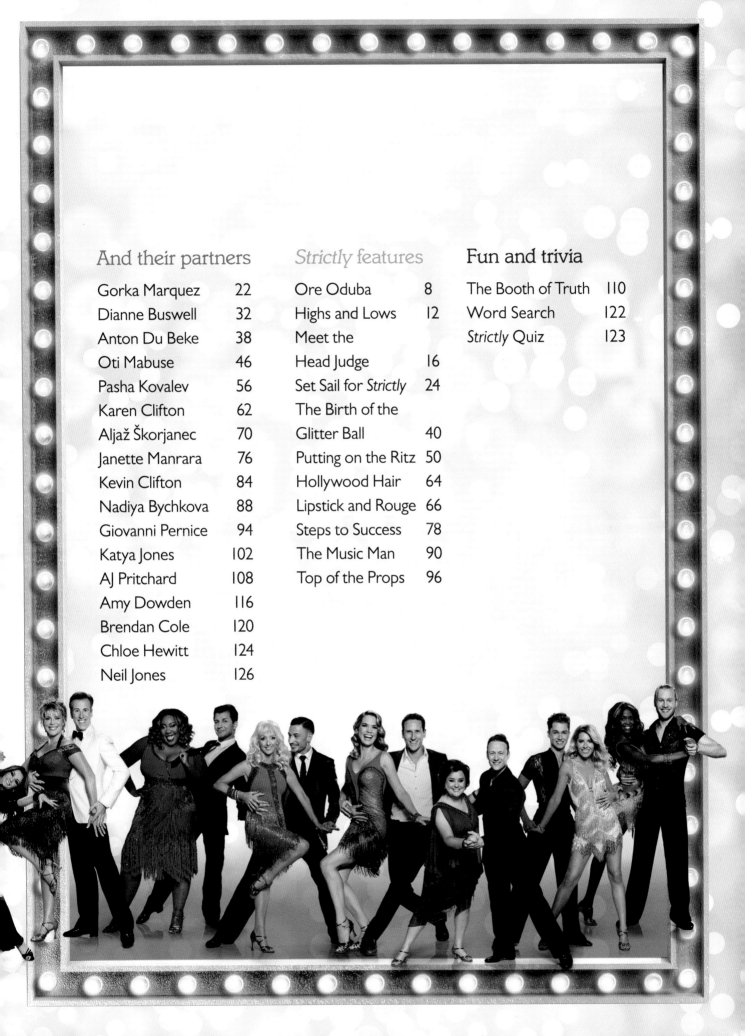

Tess Daly

Since presenting the first show, Tess has seen 14 sets of celebrities shimmying across the *Strictly* floor. But she thinks the class of 2017 are the boldest yet.

'Even at the red-carpet launch I noticed that they were hardly a shy and retiring bunch,' she said. 'It was their first foray under the *Strictly* spotlight, but they were really going for it. I have high hopes for them.'

The eagerness spilled over into the launch show, when they were paired with the *Strictly* professionals.

'I've never seen such enthusiasm from the celebrities when they were matched with their partners,' laughs Tess. 'Ruth Langsford said it all when she threw herself into Anton's arms so enthusiastically! Susan was overwhelmed because she adores Kevin so much – she has his photo on her fridge – and she cried genuine tears when they were paired up. But they all seem ready to throw themselves in at full throttle.'

Tess reveals she and co-presenter Claudia stand at the side of the stage during the celebrities' first group dance 'spotting the runners and riders.'

'Aston's done break-dancing routines with JLS but ballroom and Latin will be a new discipline. Alexandra and Debbie are looking good. Debbie has a ballet background and even though she hasn't danced for a long time, I think she will surprise people because she's got rhythm and poise.

'Then there is the Reverend Richard Coles, who had me in hysterics behind the scenes because he has the wickedest sense of humour. He wants to throw himself into the whole process and he's completely up for the Lycra, sequin and fake-tan experience.

'Paralympian Jonnie Peacock seems quite shy, which is endearing, and he has Oti, who is an incredible choreographer, so they could be a dynamite couple. He's incredibly fit and watching him dance will be a powerful experience. He is used to winning medals and is incredibly competitive and he will have the stamina for the training which is hugely important.

'We haven't had a female winner since 2014, with Caroline Flack, but this year the ladies are looking pretty strong.'

After watching new judge Shirley Ballas on the launch show, Tess is expecting her to make quite an impact.

'Shirley had a strong debut,' she says. 'She had huge shoes to fill with Len, who has been there since day one, but Claudia and I fell in love with Shirley the moment we met her. She's warm, she's witty, she's had an incredible career and she's been a judge, so her credentials are unshakable. Welcome to the family, Shirley.'

The launch show also had a poignant side for Tess, who shed a tear after the tribute to former co-presenter Bruce Forsyth, who passed away in August.

'It was overwhelming because I knew that Bruce's family were watching,' she reveals. 'I'd been with them the day before, and I was very moved by the tribute, showing what Bruce brought to the show and the magic moments we shared together. I was watching my friend up there and I felt his loss very keenly. I loved him, simple as that. When the film ended with him saying goodbye, I couldn't speak because it was like he was in the room and I knew he would have loved it. There wasn't a dry eye in the house.

'Viewers have told me they shed a tear because he entertained the nation for seven decades so we'll all miss him. But I have no doubt that he'd want us all to "Keeep dancing."'

Ore Oduba

A Sporting Dance

Almost a year on from lifting the trophy, *Strictly* champ Ore Oduba is still reeling from the shock.

'It was just surreal,' he says. 'I have watched that moment back a few times but it still doesn't make any sense. Before the result, I can honestly say that I was thinking about raising the other couple on our shoulders and getting to the bar. When Tess said our names, our jaws dropped to the floor and it took us about eight seconds to register what had just happened.'

Although Ore danced like a dream in the final, and won huge praise from the judges, things were touch and go backstage just before he took to the floor. 'I got terrible cramp in my thighs after the dress rehearsal,' he explains. 'About an hour before the final I was sitting with my legs in the air, eating bananas, and trying anything I could to get rid of it. But we had three incredible routines and I wanted to make a fitting end to a phenomenal series.'

Before taking on the *Strictly* challenge, as a BBC *Breakfast* presenter Ore was more at home on a sofa than on a dance floor. But, despite having no previous dance experience, the sports reporter was hiding a secret passion.

'None of my friends and family, or even my wife, knew the passion I had for this programme,' he explains. 'This was deep-rooted. I had been watching it for 12 years, religiously, so the thought I would one day be on it was a dream. I was determined to go in at full throttle.'

The presenter was paired with Joanne Clifton at the launch show and he says she was the perfect teacher for him.

'We were in sync from the first second. We have the same sense of humour and I didn't

A spectacular final saw Ore and Joanne crowned *Strictly* champs for 2016.

Geronimo! Ore burst onto the scene with a terrific tango in week 1.

have a dance style but, as I found out quickly, her dance style was right up my street. I was so keen to learn and soak up all her knowledge and she was a superb teacher.'

Ore didn't take long to catch on. In week 3, he danced up a storm with his now iconic American smooth, to *Singin' in the Rain*.

'That's when it all started piecing together,' he recalls. 'Two days before the live show, we recorded the routine and Jo watched it back and started crying. I thought I was doing pretty well but I couldn't see what she was seeing as a coach, which was her pupil growing into a dancer.'

The elegant routine included one tricky move that had Ore worried – flipping and catching an umbrella. 'I had that umbrella with me every hour of the day that week,' he laughs. 'I was flipping at work, at home and walking along the street because I knew if I dropped it that could be a ten turned into a two.

> 'Jo and I hugged in the middle of the floor, and I thought "This is real."'

'On the night of the show, I flipped the umbrella, caught it, ended the routine and the audience just erupted. I could feel the emotion of the room, Jo and I hugged in the middle of the floor, and I thought "This is real." We had

Ore made a splash with his American smooth to *Singin' in the Rain*.

come into our own and I think that's when we became contenders.'

The judges scored the couple 35, with Len comparing Ore to Gene Kelly – and he wasn't the only one who thought so.

'Gene Kelly's widow Patricia sent me and Joanne a message, which is when it got really surreal,' reveals Ore. 'She called it a "beautiful tribute", adding that Gene had never wanted anyone to impersonate him but to use his work as an inspiration and that he would have been proud. It was incredible, first that she was watching and secondly that she thought it was good enough that she wanted to personally message us.'

The American smooth got a second outing in the Grand Final, scoring 39, along with a stunning show dance and a jive, which both achieved a perfect score and won Ore and Joanne the *Strictly* crown.

'It was a special moment and to have enjoyed it with friends and family, and my wife Portia watching, and to be there with Jo who had given me this wonderful gift of dance, was incredible,' says Ore. 'I had always dreamed of being part of the show, and living it was better than I could have dreamed.'

HIGHS and LOWS

Just when you think the dancing can't get any better, every *Strictly* series see a new benchmark set and a new record broken. But not every dance can be a triumph and someone has to be bottom of the leader board for each dance. Step in to our record-breaking Hall of Fame.

THE HIGHS

Until last year, series 12 champ Caroline Flack had the most perfect scores with four but she's now been matched by series 14 runner-up Danny Mac.

Danny and partner Oti Mabuse became the first couple ever to be awarded a 40 for the samba, with their African-inspired routine in series 14. The rumba is now the only dance where the first perfect score is still up for grabs

The record for the highest averag Natalie Gumede, with 36.87 but Da snapping at her heels, with 36.63.

Ore Oduba and Joanne Clifton ar couple to match the record for the j Jill Halfpenny and Darren Bennett in was the first celebrity to score a pe

THE LOWS

Ann Widdecombe holds the record most low scores with three to her n the salsa, samba and American smoo highest score was 21 and her lowest salsa, was 12.

Quentin Willson still holds the re lowest score ever with an 8 (1, 1, 3, series 2 cha-cha.

HIGHEST SCORES

American Smooth
- [40] Ali Bastian & Brian Fortuna
- [40] Natalie Gumede & Artem Chigvintsev

Argentine tango
- [40] Jason Donovan & Kristina Rihanoff
- [40] Harry Judd & Aliona Vilani
- [40] Simon Webbe & Kristina Rihanoff
- [40] Louise Redknapp & Kevin Clifton

Cha-cha-cha
- [40] Lisa Snowdon & Brendan Cole
- [40] Caroline Flack & Pasha Kovalev

Charleston
- [40] Chris Hollins & Ola Jordan
- [40] Kimberley Walsh & Pasha Kovalev
- [40] Denise van Outen & James Jordan
- [40] Caroline Flack & Pasha Kovalev

- [40] Georgia May Foote & Giovanni Pernice
- [40] Danny Mac & Oti Mabuse

Foxtrot
- [40] Rachel Stevens & Vincent Simone
- [40] Lisa Snowdon & Brendan Cole

Jive
- [40] Jill Halfpenny & Darren Bennett
- [40] Ore Oduba & Joanne Clifton

Paso doble
- [40] Chelsee Healey & Pasha Kovalev

Quickstep
- [40] Lisa Snowdon & Brendan Cole
- [40] Ricky Whittle & Natalie Lowe
- [40] Pamela Stephenson & James Jordan
- [40] Harry Judd & Aliona Vilani

Rumba
- [39] Rachel Stevens & Vincent Simone
- [39] Kara Tointon & Artem Chigvintsev
- [39] Chelsee Healey & Pasha Kovalev
- [39] Jay McGuiness & Aliona Vilani

Salsa
- [40] Mark Ramprakash & Karen Hardy
- [40] Abbey Clancy & Aljaž Skorjanec
- [40] Natalie Gumede & Artem Chigvintsev
- [40] Caroline Flack & Pasha Kovalev

Samba
- [40] Danny Mac & Oti Mabuse

Show dance
- [40] Jason Donovan & Kristina Rihanoff
- [40] Denise van Outen & James Jordan

- [40] Louis Smith & Flavia Cacace
- [40] Natalie Gumede & Artem Chigvintsev
- [40] Caroline Flack & Pasha Kovalev
- [40] Kellie Bright & Kevin Clifton
- [40] Ore Oduba & Joanne Clifton
- [40] Danny Mac & Oti Mabuse

Tango
- [40] Kimberley Walsh & Pasha Kovalev
- [40] Kellie Bright & Kevin Clifton

Viennese waltz
- [40] Ali Bastian & Brian Fortuna
- [40] Pamela Stephenson & James Jordan

Waltz
- [40] Matt Di Angelo & Flavia Cacace
- [40] Abbey Clancy & Aljaž Skorjanec

LOWEST SCORES

American Smooth

[14] Ann Widdecombe & Anton du Beke

Argentine tango

[26] Colin Salmon & Kristina Rihanoff

[26] Michael Vaughan & Natalie Lowe

Cha-cha-cha

[8] Quentin Willson & Hazel Newberry

Charleston

[13] Tony Jacklin & Aliona Vilani

Foxtrot

[17] Richard Arnold & Erin Boag

Jive

[15] Michael Vaughan & Natalie Lowe

Paso doble

[15] Christopher Parker & Hanna Karttunen

[15] Dennis Taylor & Izabela Hannah

Quickstep

[12] Diarmuid Gavin & Nicole Cutler

Rumba

[13] Fiona Phillips & Brendan Cole

[13] Carol Kirkwood & Pasha Kovalev

Salsa

[12] Ann Widdecombe & Anton du Beke

Samba

[13] Ann Widdecombe & Anton du Beke

Show dance

[22] Christopher Parker & Hanna Karttunen

Tango

[14] Diarmuid Gavin & Nicole Cutler

Viennese waltz

[21] Carol Kirkwood & Pasha Kovalev

Waltz

[11] Fiona Phillips & Brendan Cole

Meet the HEAD JUDGE

This year's *Strictly* sees a glamorous new addition to the judges' panel, in the shape of new head judge Shirley Ballas. The former world champion Latin dancer replaces Len Goodman on the desk and it seems the Fearsome Foursome just got feistier.

'I'm all about the four Fs – I'll be fun, firm, feisty but fair,' she jokes. 'I'm quite strict but I wouldn't expect anything from them that I wouldn't expect from myself. I want great determination, beautiful work ethic, and I love a person who is willing to come in week after week and not be nervous, who will try anything, and is ready to listen to those technical things that will really benefit them.'

Shirley grew up in Wallasey, Merseyside, and started dancing at the age of seven.

'I was at St Chad's Church at the Brownies and there was a dance class happening on the other side of the door,' she recalls. 'I looked through the window and saw everybody doing a cha cha cha and I was hooked. I asked the gentleman whether he would do any children's classes and he said, "Funnily enough, we start on Saturday." I never missed a lesson. Sunshine, hail, sleet, I went every week.'

At eight she began competing in local contests at the Capitol Ballroom in Liscard, partnered by another girl, Irene Hamilton. 'I loved it straight away,' she says. 'I still have the first tiny cup that I won, that my mother is very proud of, and my first medals.'

She went on to become three-time British

Open to the World Latin American Champion and 10-time United States Latin American Champion, as well as winning multiple British National Championship titles. Accustomed as she is to winning, she knows how it feels to be judged along the way.

'I moved to the US when I was 23, and my partner, Corky Ballas, was a beginner so I had to train him,' she reveals. 'But we came back to win the title in 1995, so perseverance and determination are a huge part of what I have myself and what I'll be looking for in the contestants.'

'The Queen of Latin' retired from competitive dancing in 1996 and is now an acclaimed international coach to many of the top professional and amateur dancers as well as a sought-after judge for ballroom and Latin American competitions all around the world – all skills she will bring to her new role in *Strictly*.

'I teach dancing and I adjudicate all over the world so I have to spot things in a flash,' she says. 'You get a split second to make a decision, so when the first few bars of music play I'll be able to tell what's going on.'

Shirley Ballas

Head judge Shirley is looking forward to 'getting to know people' on the show but says her fellow judges have already made her feel at home.

'I've known Bruno for 10 years, Craig is a sweetheart and Darcey is just beautiful, so I think with the judges' group it's going to be great,' she said. 'I couldn't have asked for a better welcome than I got from them. Craig even sent me flowers for my birthday the day after the launch show, so I was very impressed.'

Shirley's first experience in the judge's chair was at the launch show, which she says was 'spectacular and amazing'.

'It was truly an experience. I had some butterflies in my tummy but I think it was more out of anticipation than nerves. I can't wait to watch everybody's journey on *Strictly* from week to week. As the new head judge, I'll be expecting some different things from them so it's going to be exciting.'

Why did you want to join *Strictly*?

My son Mark is a pro dancer on *Dancing with the Stars* in the United States and when Len mentioned that he wanted to step aside, Mark said, 'Why don't you try for it?' I did a screen test and I ended up getting the job and my whole life changed. I love the show because it brings glitz and glamour to a Saturday evening in front of the TV. It brings journeys that people can relate to, watching people struggle and then coming to the forefront, maybe the underdog making it to the final. It's an exciting show on all levels.

What are you looking for in a contestant?

I'm looking for great grounding through the floor, with good balance. I'm looking for synchronisation, how they interact their arms with their legs. Do they have any chemistry with their partner? Are they someone who will think outside the box? Plus musicality, how they are going to translate the music with their body?

Will you be a stickler for the rules?

My nature as a person is that I stick to the rules, so if you tell me you must do 'this, this and this', I will do it. If you tell me I have to be there at five o'clock, I'm there at quarter to five. I'm a very rule-oriented person myself and I like to be corrected if I've made a mistake. That's my nature, so I will be attracted to that in other people.

Who do you have your eye on?

I've got my beady eye on all of them. They all surprised me at the launch show, and I wouldn't want to pick out anyone in particular. They came down that set of stairs and they all looked amazing.

Do you think they will give you any lip?

In the heat of the moment, when the pressure is on, you never know, but looking at them I don't think so. They look like lovely people. At the end of the day, my job is to critique exactly what I see, so I have to do that. I have done it for 50 years, I'm trained in it, I've had it done to myself over my own career and people took no prisoners. But I want to give the contestants something that they can hold on to, week after week, and improve their dancing.

Do you have a favourite dance?

I love traditional ballroom dances, like the Viennese waltz, but I also love the rumba and the Argentine tango. I love the skill and the music in the rumba and it's so slow. You can often tell an amazing dancer by the way they dance the rumba and move slowly to the music.

Alexandra Burke

She famously sang about *Broken Heels* in one of her biggest hits but Alexandra is struggling to cope with any heels at all in her *Strictly* training.

'Because I played a nun for a year in *Sister Act: The Musical* wearing flat shoes, I've been trying to wear heels just to give my ankles a bit more strength,' she reveals. 'I found it difficult because I'm always in the gym, I'm always wearing trainers or flats, and all of a sudden I'm elevated, but I'm hoping for the best.'

The London-born singer rose to fame in the 2008 series of *The X Factor*, alongside Aston Merrygold's band JLS. But she is happy to be going head to head with her old rival on the dance floor.

'Aston and I have a special relationship,' she says. 'He is my comfort and my support. It's great to have somebody there who is my friend and I'm rooting for that man 100 per cent.

'At the end of the day, we're there to support each other and we have been since the beginning.'

To make time for the show Alexandra, whose debut single *Hallelujah* sold over a million copies and became the biggest seller of 2008, has temporarily shelved plans to record a new album.

'My mum always said to me, "Be great at one thing, and the rest will follow." When I was doing *X Factor*, she made me stop dancing and acting and said acting will follow and eight years later, I was in *The Bodyguard* and *Sister Act* so she wasn't wrong. Then she said dancing will follow and now it has. The three things I love more than anything in the world are singing, dancing and acting, and here I am doing one of those three things.'

While she is used to performing onstage, Alexandra says she will still have jangling nerves on a Saturday night.

'What makes me nervous is that even though it's a stage and I'm wearing a glamorous outfit – I am not singing,' she admits. 'I'm completely out of my comfort zone without a microphone in my hand and I can't rely on a mic stand to do a move if something goes wrong!

'It's scary but it's my dream show. I still have to pinch myself, because this is a once-in-a-lifetime opportunity and I'm never going to get this moment back.'

Spanish dancer Gorka was fresh to the *Strictly* floor last year, but was knocked out in week 3 with *EastEnders* star Tameka Empson. For his second series, with singer Alexandra Burke, he is hoping to go all the way to the Grand Final.

'Alexandra has a lot of potential and she is very talented,' he says. 'But it's not only about how good you are at dancing, there are so many other factors. I will do my best. Fingers crossed.'

Although he said was surprised to be paired with the *Broken Heels* singer, he was thrilled when he realised they were the last two standing after all the other couples were matched up on the launch show.

'I couldn't believe it,' he says. 'It was a wonderful surprise. We got on well as soon as we met. We were telling each other jokes and we had a good vibe as soon as we practised together.

'I'm very excited. She is a beautiful person and she's very hard working. In training, I'll tell her, "Let's leave it there", and she'll say, "No, let's do it one more time." She has so much commitment.'

Although the Bilbao-born dancer admits that Alexandra's musical background is a bonus, he says it can only help up to a point.

'People who come from a music background can often dance and feel comfortable on the stage, and it can help them to learn quickly, but ballroom and Latin are completely different techniques and a different way to move your body. Dancing on pop videos doesn't mean you will be a good ballroom or Latin dancer.'

Gorka began dancing at the age of 12 and represented Spain in the World Latin Championships in 2010 before reaching the semi-finals of the 2012 WDSF World Cup.

Despite the early exit, Gorka says he loved dancing with actress Tameka on his debut and he had a fabulous year.

'I loved Tameka,' he says. 'She helped me so much and taught me so much. We didn't get to do enough and we had so much more to show to everyone.

'But my first year on the show was amazing. It was like a dream come true. I kept pinching myself and thinking that a lot of dancers would love to be in my place, it's such a fantastic opportunity.

'At the same time, it was like a new world and there was so much to take in. When I met all of the other dancers, then the celebrities, I was in awe, and then I went to the studio I was like, "Wow, what is this?" Everything was huge in every way – the cameras, the audience, the dances, everything.

'I had a fabulous year, but I think this year I am going to enjoy it even more because I know what is going on around me.'

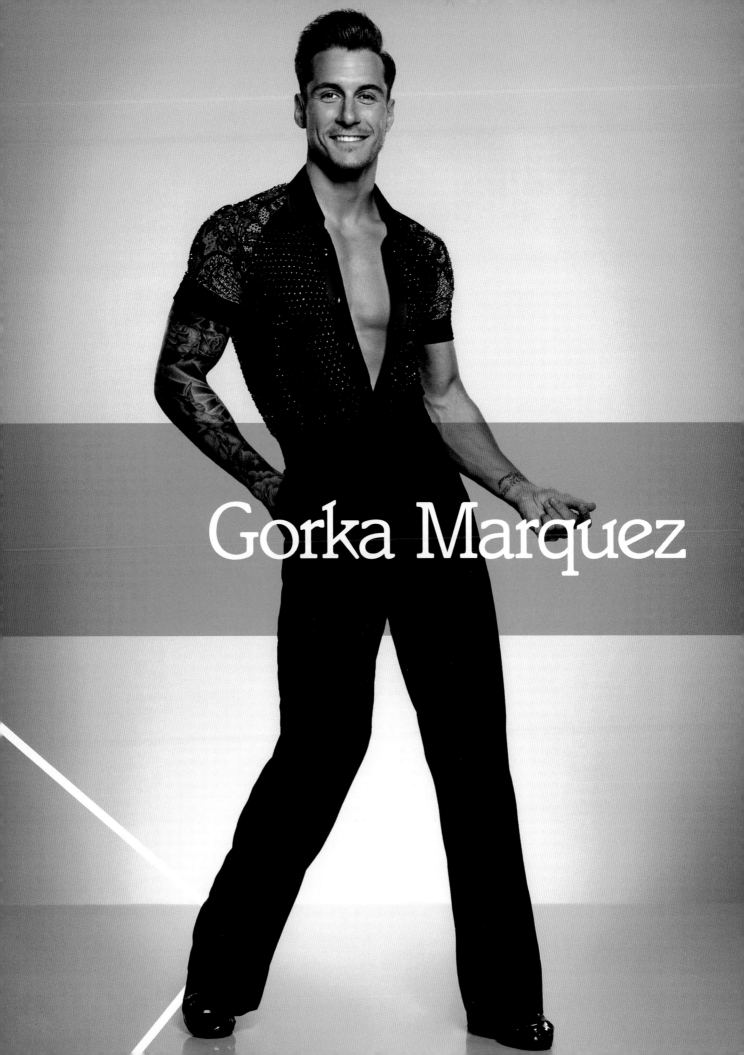

Gorka Marquez

SET SAIL for STRICTLY

In the months before it returns to our screens for its autumn run, *Strictly Come Dancing* packs up the sequins and takes to the high seas. On board the *Strictly*-themed cruises, which have been running for five years, guests rub shoulders with judges and professional dancers as they waltz their way around the Mediterranean.

For the professionals, it's a chance to get closer to the fans of the show.

'I love the fact that we can talk to the fans and find out what they think about us and about the show,' says Giovanni Pernice. 'You can feel the love.'

'We don't get to meet the fans very often,' says Janette Manrara. 'But on the ship you get to say "hi", meet them at breakfast and at the Q&As. It's nice to get to chat to them.'

This June saw the *Britannia* head for St

Petersburg and the Baltic states with Craig Revel Horwood, Janette and Aljaž, Giovanni, Oti and Oksana on board. But while the pro dancers have a ball, it is far from a holiday. As well as hosting dance classes and taking part in Q&As with the guests, each pair puts on four dance showcases and rehearsals start as soon as they get on board.

'The dancers put on great shows and the guests get to see them performing up close,' says executive producer of the cruise shows Richard Curwen. 'The day we embark, we immediately start rehearsals and we rehearse solidly for three days while they host masterclasses and have meet and greets in between.

'The pros usually have their dances choreographed beforehand, but they have to learn the space, then we add more content. So, for instance, the ship's dance instructors appear as support dancers and they have to be choreographed in and learn the routines. We use the ship's production team so they are learning the show as we go too.'

For Richard, each cruise is a year in the planning and he starts booking dancers as soon as the TV show's line-up is confirmed.

'We want the shows to have a different feel and cover the breadth of skills and styles that we cover in the TV show,' he says. 'It's wonderful for fans to see the dancers perform.'

In preparation for the showcases, Richard works with dance producer Kim Winston and the ship's entertainment manager to make sure everything is shipshape. But life on the ocean waves doesn't always run to plan.

'Weather can mean we arrive at port late or divert,' explains Richard. 'Or it could be so rocky that you can't put a show on. We've only had to cancel a show once for safety reasons. I asked Natalie Lowe to do a rumba walk for me and she went sailing off into the wings, so I thought we'd better cancel!'

When the show does go on, it provides a magnificent spectacle for the dance lovers on board. Janette and Aljaž whip through the waltz, a jive and a stunning American smooth while Oti and Giovanni get the party started with a saucy samba and dramatic paso.

At the masterclasses run by the *Strictly* pro dancers many of the guests prove that they already know their way around the dance floor. Each class is heaving with talented amateurs, eager to hone their skills.

'They come on board and take the lessons and they do get better,' says Janette. 'They pick up new steps and new moves and they look really good.'

'Our cha-cha-cha masterclass was absolutely packed,' adds Aljaž. 'I love the fact that so many people are on board because they love dancing and they love *Strictly*. It's brilliant.'

STRICTLY AT SEA

Some of the braver dancers among the ship's guests take on the *Strictly* challenge for real – competing against other couples for a glitter ball trophy and an elusive 10. In total, 10 couples compete in two shows judged by Craig, the ship's Captain and one of the professional dancers. And Craig's sharp tongue doesn't get any softer just because he's at sea.

'I'm even more critical than I am on the show,' he admits. 'But people love being told the truth and they expect it. I think everyone would be very disappointed if I came on and said, "You're all marvellous, darling. 10,10,10,10."

'On this cruise, a lady came up to me and said, "Do you remember me from the last cruise? You said your floorboards had more movement that my hips!" I did remember her.

She worked solidly for two weeks on a dance, only to be given a 1 by me. But she was laughing and saw the humour.'

The contestants in the on-board *Strictly*-themed competition show go through heats to get to the final. Among the couples lining up for the second *Strictly* guest competition on the 2017 *Britannia* cruise were two couples celebrating 35 years of marriage and one couple, Doreen and Adrian, who had travelled from Malta to the UK to join the ship for their 25th wedding anniversary.

The winners of the show, however, were Birmingham newlyweds David and Adam Shaw – whose energetic dance to *Crazy In Love* bagged them a perfect score. Craig told them, 'I loved the acrobatics. Fantastic.' Amazingly, they had only been dancing for two weeks.

'We do amateur theatre at home but we've never done ballroom before,' said David. 'But we love the show so much and we saw they were doing heats so we thought we'd give it a go. We auditioned with a cha-cha but it wasn't quite right and when we saw the demonstration with Janette and Aljaž we realised that our cha-cha was actually a salsa. So we had a couple of crash classes and here we are.'

DECKED OUT

No *Strictly* event would be complete without the sparkle – and there's plenty of that on board. In fact, 48 of the costumes from the previous series travel on the cruise and are displayed on 16 mannequins dotted through the atrium of the ship.

Many guests join a costume tour with Theresa Hewlett, studio manager from dress designer DSI, who work closely with *Strictly*'s designer Vicky Gill. Dresses are hired from DSI for the Saturday night TV shows, then altered and embellished by Vicky and her team. Theresa also oversees the last-minute alterations behind the scenes.

'The guests love hearing how the dresses are made,' she says. 'Many of them make their own clothes and know how to sew and they love to look up close. At first they think they are not allowed to touch but I say, "Lift the skirt up and have a look" because that's what they're there for.

'A lot of them are interested in the crinoline hems, which stiffen the hemline, because until you point it out they don't know it's there. They are also interested in the structure, because we construct them around leotards so that the wearer is really safe in the dress. They also love to chat to someone who has been in the *Strictly* studio, and knows what goes on backstage.'

Among the favourites this year were Natalie Lowe's wine-coloured medieval design, from her American smooth with Greg Rutherford, Oti Mabuse's stoned show-dance dress, from her final routine with Danny Mac, and Joanne Clifton's Hells Angels-inspired quickstep dress, with leather-look panels.

> 'The guests love hearing how the dresses are made.'

'This was the worst dress to make,' Theresa jokes. 'It has wet-look Lycra, satin and georgette, plus zips and a mesh front, and the stretchy fabrics were fighting with the non-stretchy fabrics. It took me three days to make it.'

As well as being displayed on the ship, the costumes are given an outing on the catwalk, modelled by the ship's dance troupe and some male crew members.

'We have eight or nine dresses in each show,' explains DSI sales manager Carole Williams. 'And we change the mannequin display after each fashion show so the guests get to see as many dresses as possible. It's wonderful to watch the fans' reaction to the costumes because it's a rare chance to get that close.'

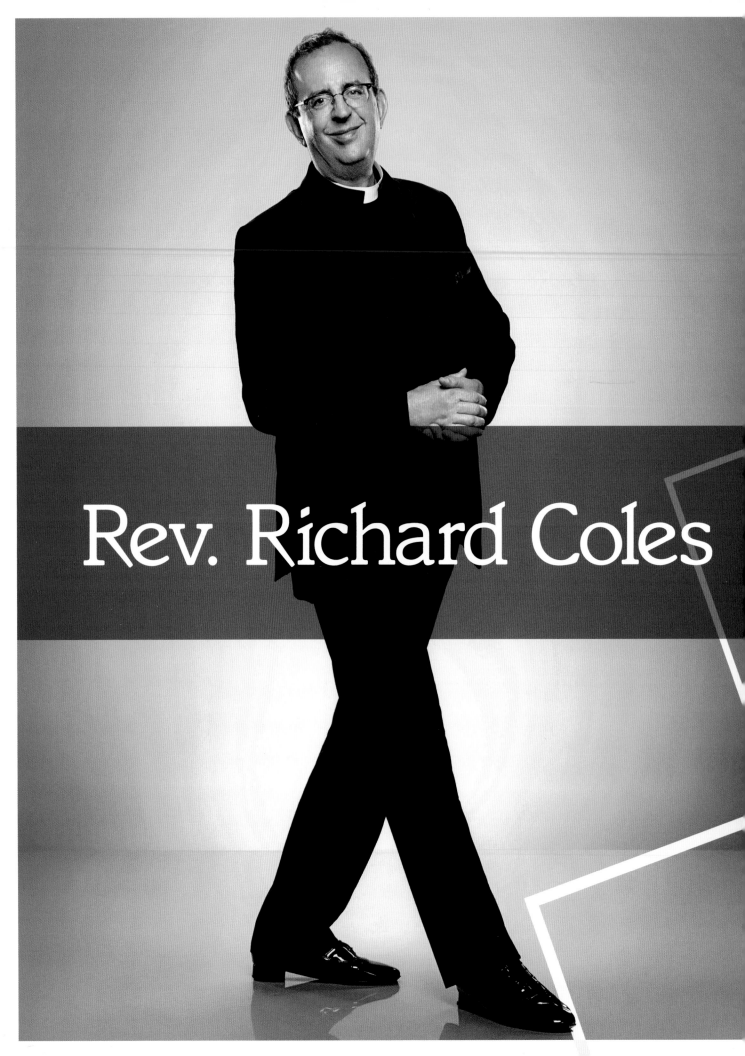

Rev. Richard Coles

The seasoned broadcaster is the first man of the cloth to grace the *Strictly* dance floor but he can't wait to show off his heavenly moves.

'I'm just amazed that it took them 15 series to decide on me,' he jokes. 'I've been waiting by the phone for over a decade and then the call came and I thought very carefully about it – for about 1.2 seconds! I know some people who have done it and they all said they had a fantastic time.'

Although he has no real dance experience, the Rev does have a musical background. He first shot to fame as one half of The Communards, with singer Jimmy Somerville, scoring three top-ten hits including *Don't Leave Me This Way*, the biggest single of 1986. The Nottingham-born musician turned to religion after studying theology at King's College London, and became an ordained Anglican vicar in 2005. He has since carved out a distinguished broadcasting career, fronting Radio 4's *Saturday Live* as well as appearing on TV shows including *Celebrity Masterchef* and *Songs of Praise*.

Richard insists he is from the 'David Brent school of dance', but adds, 'People like David Brent so that might help.'

He admits that dancing was not his forte, even in the heady days of pop stardom.

'I was standing at the back in the dark, not even gyrating,' he says. 'I performed with Jimmy Somerville, who was not only a brilliant singer but a brilliant dancer too. So 30 years later the time has come to release my moves.'

The Reverend is particularly looking forward to dancing the Argentine tango. 'If you're a vicar you are rather austere,' he says. 'So I like the idea of having a sizzling dance.'

As well as showing off his steps, Richard is happy to swap his dog collar for glitter and sequins.

'Obviously in a cassock, I sizzle,' he jokes. 'I'll keep my shirt on. But if you're going to do it I think you have to really throw yourself into it and go the whole hog.

'I'm very excited about the spray tan. There was a knock on the door last night from a member of my parochial church council and I said, "I can't come to the door. I'm exfoliating!" I've never exfoliated before.'

Richard admits to being a 'competitive person' but believes there will be some challenges ahead if he is to lift the glitter ball.

'Remembering more than two things at once will be my biggest worry, especially in the quick dances,' he laughs. 'But my biggest challenge will be not being helicoptered to A&E. To get through the series without scrambling in a hospital helicopter, that would be good!'

Australian dancer Dianne joins the *Strictly* cast after a year on the Australian version of the show, *Dancing with the Stars*, and she can't wait to take her first steps on the UK dance floor.

'I'm over the moon,' she says. 'It's what every dancer dreams of and it's a one-in-a-million chance. I just want to do the best job I can and prove I'm here for a reason.

'I had an amazing experience on the Australian show. I absolutely loved it and ever since then I've been wanting to do another series. I love the fact that you start with someone who can't dance and at the end of it they can dance, and they really enjoy it so it's very rewarding.'

Dianne started dancing at five in her home town of Bunbury, Australia, as she wanted to follow in her brother Andrew's footsteps.

'My brother, who is older than me, has danced his whole life so I grew up going to the studios,' she reveals. 'We would drop him off at lessons and I would see the dancing and I'd say to Mum, "I want to do this" and so I got into it as well. Andrew is an Australian champion and a dance teacher and he's coming over for my first

two *Strictly* shows. He's my biggest fan.'

Dianne's passion for dance led her to become an Australian Open Champion and four-time Amateur Australian Open Finalist. In her first year on *Strictly*, she is partnered with the Reverend Richard Coles – and it seems she is spending as much time rolling around the floor with the giggles as she is dancing.

'I'm having an amazing time,' she says. 'His schedule is full on, so I've been up to Glasgow, we've come back to London and there's bits and pieces everywhere but I'm really enjoying it.

'He is very funny and every day there's a point when I'm on the floor crying with laughter. He will be great fun to watch.

'At the beginning, I thought this was going to take a while, and I had to tell myself that he had never danced before in his life,' she admits. 'But by day four the improvement was amazing.'

Dianne, one of three new professionals joining the team this year, says she won't be suffering from nerves on her first foray onto the *Strictly* floor – at least not on her own behalf.

'I personally don't get too nervous, but I might be a little nervous for Richard, so my thoughts are completely with him,' she says. 'I have danced my whole life so for me to do a routine is natural but for him it is a big deal.'

Dianne Buswell

Craig Revel Horwood

Craig Revel Horwood has been a fixture in the *Strictly* ballroom since the show began. As the new batch of hopefuls head to the hallowed dance floor, he's expecting this series to be even more fab-u-lous.

'I'm looking forward to working with Shirley Ballas,' he says. 'I think she will enlighten us all with her comments, and I'm really looking forward to the dancing. We have an amazing group of people and I'm hoping they will all buckle down and enjoy the ride as much as the judges.'

However, the sharp-tongued judge has a word of warning for contestants looking for an easy ride. 'I'm going to be the toughest I've ever been. I'm going to stand for nothing!'

What do you think of the line-up?

It's one of the best years. There's a great cross section of people. I think Aston Merrygold has the potential to wow the audience and could go to heights beyond even Danny Mac. Alexandra could take well to it, because she has musical talents, and hopefully she will have the wow factor.

Any other names stand out for you?

I'm excited to have our first Paralympian in Jonnie Peacock. Jonnie is certainly fit enough, and he's used to overcoming obstacles to become a champion, so he will have the right mindset.

Brian Conley will be one to watch because he's like an old-fashioned song-and-dance man. I don't know if he has any technique but he won't be afraid to speak his mind, so we might have words!

Who do you think will make us laugh on the dance floor?

Susan Calman will bring some quality humour to the show but I think Debbie McGee is characterful and funny. I'm looking forward to the Reverend Richard Coles. We've never had a vicar before and as a former musician he should do reasonably well.

Are you looking forward to having Shirley at the judges' desk?

Shirley is the most qualified person on the panel, having won Latin championships in the US and the UK, and she knows her stuff. She will also be able to provide a lot of technical know-how. But she's opinionated too, so I'm looking forward to our disagreements.

What did you think of last year's final?

It was amazing, like watching professional dancers. My favourite dance of the series was Danny Mac's Charleston – I loved that.

What are your favourite memories of Bruce Forsyth?

Bruce was a gorgeous human being who was very genuine, loving and caring with all the company. He was a real father figure for all of us on the show and a legend, so his legacy will live on for many years. He will be sadly missed.

Ruth Langsford

Daytime TV presenter Ruth is keen to learn as many dances as she can during her *Strictly* stint but there is one routine that she particularly wants to perform – for a very special reason.

'I'm looking forward to all of the dances but the jive particularly, because my parents were really good at the jive,' she says. 'It always fascinated me that that generation could go to a dance and whoever asked them to dance, they could do a jive. I loved watching my parents jive.'

The *Loose Women* star, who also hosts *This Morning* with husband Eamonn Holmes, started life in Singapore in 1960, moving to five different countries before the age of ten with her parents Dennis and Joan. She started her broadcasting career as a continuity announcer on a local TV station in South-West England before moving to ITV to present a variety of shows and becoming a permanent anchor on *Loose Women*.

For Ruth, being asked to do *Strictly Come Dancing* is a dream come true.

'This has been on my fantasy to-do list and I've made no bones about that,' she admits. 'When anyone asked me which reality show I would like to do, I always say *Strictly*, thinking they would see that and ask me. So when I was finally asked it was an opportunity I couldn't let pass me by.

'One thing I love about *Strictly* is when people surprise you. It takes people who you can't imagine dancing in their everyday jobs and then suddenly you see these dancers blossom. I'm a huge fan of the show and I love that families watch it together and everyone has an opinion about who their favourite dancer is.'

While Eamonn has encouraged her to unleash her inner dancer on the show, he won't be joining her on the dance floor any time soon. Instead, she is relying on their 15-year-old son Jack to put her through her paces at home.

'Jack is surprisingly encouraging. I did worry that, at 15, he might find it awkward at school but he loves music and he plays the drums, so he is the one who has been practising the steps with me. Eamonn is more concerned about how he is going to get to the football on a Saturday and come and watch me on *Strictly*.'

The TV star has also found plenty of support from her loyal daytime audience, and says she is keen to show that older women can strut their stuff.

'The women who watch *This Morning* and *Loose Women*, and the women who follow me on social media, are predominantly women of my age group and they all seem to be thrilled. They're all saying, "We're right behind you on this", so I do feel I'm doing it for the more mature women of Britain.'

Anton has been a fan favourite since he first took to the *Strictly* dance floor with opera star Lesley Garrett in series 1. As one of two original professionals, along with Brendan Cole, his witty and memorable routines with such partners as Ann Widdecombe, Judy Murray and Nancy Dell'Olio have made him very popular – not least with new partner Ruth Langsford's mum.

This Morning presenter Ruth was over the moon to be paired with the ballroom king at the launch show and revealed, 'My mum loves Anton.' For his part, Anton is thrilled with his new dance partner.

'Ruth and I are going to have a great time,' he says. 'She is absolutely tremendous. I can't wait.'

Anton grew up in Sevenoaks, Kent. A talented junior boxer and footballer, he came to dancing at the relatively late age of 14, and studied contemporary, jazz, ballet and modern theatre dance until, inspired by his idol Fred Astaire, he decided to specialise in ballroom.

In 1997, Anton formed a dance partnership with Erin Boag, and within a year they had become New Zealand Champions – successfully retaining their title the following year. After seven years of competing, they both joined *Strictly* for the first series in 2004 and, although Erin left after series 10, they continue to dance together.

Some of Anton's most iconic routines were performed in 2010, with former minister Ann Widdecombe, who made it to the quarter-final on the public vote. In a crowd-pleasing tango, she flew over the stage to the dance floor, prompting Bruno to name her 'Starship Widdecombe', and in another famous opening she searched for Anton in thick fog, in a *Titanic*-themed rumba.

'I've been the luckiest of the professional dancers by having the most interesting and lovely ladies to dance with over the years,' he says. 'If I hadn't danced with Ann Widdecombe that would have been my loss because she was a joy – such a scream and fun to be with.'

Anton reached the *Strictly* final in 2015, with Proms presenter Katie Derham. Last year, Anton danced with *Birds of a Feather* star Lesley Joseph, but their week 5 tango proved to be their last.

'Lesley had the potential to go much further in the competition, of that I'm sure,' he says. 'Nevertheless, what a wonderful five weeks we had dancing together on the show – truly tremendous and thoroughly good fun.'

Anton Du Beke

The birth of the GLITTER BALL

It's the glittering prize that both the celebrities and the pros are aching to get their hands on, but the famous *Strictly Come Dancing* trophy has quite a history of its own.

Back in 2004, prop makers Kier and Louise Lusby received a video of the opening titles for a new show at their Shepperton workshop.

'We played the cassette and the most amazing vision appeared,' says Louise. 'Sparkling reflections of a spinning mirrored ball with swirling colours, and the words *Strictly Come Dancing* appeared to encompass the ball, moving across its surface. It was a wonderfully exciting start to a show that gripped so many

The task given to the couple by produ[c] buyer Bobby Warans was to create an a[ ] for the winners of the sparkling new sho[w] less than a week. The starting point was[ ] inch mirror ball bought from a London [ ] that specialised in shop window displays[ ] then came the now famous *Strictly* logo.

'I looked at the graphics and my first [ ] was, "How am I going to make this look[ ] dimensional?" The letters looked like th[ ] weren't connected to the mirror ball so[ ] had to work out a way to make the rea[l] look the same,' says Louise. 'I decided t[ ] lettering would be added to clear Persp[ex] which would not be too visible, and the[ ] of the Perspex were polished so they d[ ] register too much.'

The Perspex 'handle'

curved by heating, to wrap around the ball, and was attached by clear rods to make it look like it was floating above it. The letters were cut out of brass, painted pink, and delicately added to the curved surface.

In fact, the fixed glitter ball that *Strictly* fans see at each final is not the only one Kier Lusby came up with back in 2004. 'We originally made two versions of the trophy – one with a turntable in the base driven by a motor so it turned round,' says Keir.

For the contestants, particularly those who get through to the final, the sparkling centrepiece is the holy grail of the competition.

> 'When we made the original we had no idea what a huge success the show would be.'

'The night of the final was the first time we'd seen the trophy since week one, at the launch show,' recalls 2016 champ Ore Oduba. 'At that point, you're not even considering winning it. Then to see it in the final, in front of you, is awe-inspiring.

'We all had a look at it and nobody dared to touch it, but we looked at the previous winners' names and thought it would be pretty ridiculous if our names were there. I still can't believe mine is on there.'

Although the main trophy is handed to the winning couple at the end of the series, they are given a smaller replica, with a six-inch glitter ball, to take home. The larger trophy is packed away until the following year when it is refurbished to look as good as new, and it's still going strong

after 14 years of service. There have been a few makeovers along the way. For example, the colour of the lettering has changed from pink to purple and now to gold, and there's one more vital change.

'When we made the original we had no idea what a huge success the show would be and we gave it a small square base, so there was only room for two winners' plaques per side. Once the ninth series began it had to get a new, larger base, and it ended up the same size as the original revolving one with the motor.'

In 2011 the company, Kier Lusby, closed and the couple retired, handing the reins to prop company Waterside Studios, who still make the trophies today. As well as the main trophy, they produce the two smaller prizes for the winners and two full-sized, 10-inch trophies for the live tour. They also provide the silver star trophies for the Christmas special. Unlike the mirror ball, the stars have to be individually made with each tiny bit of mirror cut to shape and stuck on by hand.

On their retirement, Kier and Louise, who had been in the prop business for 41 years, were presented with their very own gong – a lifetime achievement award from the Royal Television Society. But they still keep an eye on their iconic glitter ball.

'We both love the series and get very involved with the people,' says Louise. 'But when the winners are handed the trophy, they're terribly excited and they wave it around and, even to this day, we sit heart in mouth hoping it's not going to break or be dropped.'

It's always a nervous moment for Louise when the champions lift the glitter ball trophy.

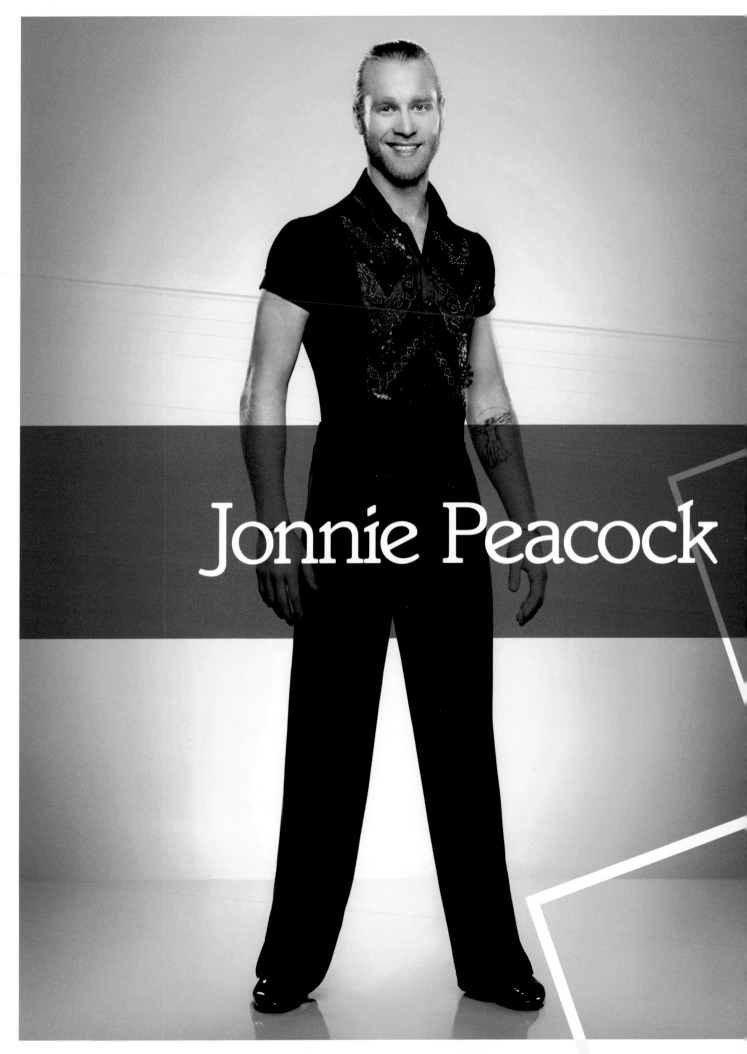
Jonnie Peacock

With two Paralympic golds to his name, Jonnie is used to winning, but when it comes to dancing, he admits he has 'low expectations'.

'I'm not thinking about the final because I don't rate myself enough to make it there,' he says modestly. 'But I think I'd be really happy if I could even get a score of 5 or 6 on the show. I'd be happy enough with that.'

While mum Linda is his biggest supporter, she didn't give him much of a vote of confidence either.

'When I told my mum she said, "No you're not! You can't dance,"' he reveals. 'I'm hoping I can prove her wrong. But she's so excited, she'll be down there at every live show.'

Born in Cambridge in 1993, Jonnie contracted meningitis at the age of five, resulting in damage to the tissue in his right leg, which had to be amputated below the knee. During a fitting for a prosthetic leg, he was directed to a Paralympic talent day and encouraged to take up athletics. At the age of 17, he broke the 100m record in para-sprinting and two years later he picked up his first Paralympic gold at the 2012 London games, repeating the feat again in Rio, in 2016.

Taking on a brand-new challenge in *Strictly*, Jonnie is thrilled to be the first amputee dancer to star in the main series.

'I think it's really exciting and it reflects the progression of the country over the last few years, since 2012 and the London Paralympics, which was great. There's a bit of pressure too, because you don't want to let anyone down but it's about changing perceptions as well. There will be a lot of people sitting at home thinking "There's no way he can ever do that," so I want to prove everybody wrong.

'I'm probably not going to be the best amputee dancer you've ever seen, and there are probably better dancers out there, but I hope it kick-starts something and gets more people involved.'

The athlete is used to tough training, so he'll take the rehearsal sessions in his stride and he's already looking forward to the live performances.

'So far every day has been a great day, everyone has been lovely, and I can't wait to get into training and get stuck in to the hard work, and feel that buzz on Saturday night.

'I grew up absolutely loving the show so it's really surreal to think that I have the opportunity to be on it. It's crazy. I'm going to look back on this experience in five years' time and still be amazed I did that.

'This is the sort of opportunity that only a handful of people ever get. To take part in the show and to be taught by someone who is absolutely at the top of their profession is wonderful. Now I'll be able to dance a little bit better on my wedding day – maybe one day.'

As a child, Oti was a talented athlete, competing in the long jump and high jump in her native South Africa. Although she turned her talents to dance, she is still a huge fan of athletics and is delighted to be going for gold with Paralympic sprinter Jonnie Peacock.

'I'm obsessed with athletics, so I'm really, really happy,' she says. 'From the moment he was announced I thought he was the one I'd like to be paired with because I have always wanted an athlete. He's so funny and we got along really well in the group rehearsals. It's a dream come true.'

As a teacher, Oti says she is after hard work and determination – as well as one other quality she believes her new partner possesses.

'He listens,' she explains. 'That's the best quality for any professional dancer. As long as your celebrity listens to you, you can create as much as you want. He pays attention and he's focused, plus he has a lot of power and strength in his body, which helps.

'He has made a point that whatever needs to be done he is going to work so hard to achieve it. I just feel so honoured and I'm excited to see how we do.'

Oti began dancing in South Africa as a young child along with her sister Motsi, who is also a professional dancer and a judge on the German version of *Strictly*. After studying for a degree in civil engineering, and becoming South African Latin American Champion eight times, Oti moved to Germany to find new challenges. She moved to the UK and joined the show in 2015 and last year she reached the final with Danny Mac, as well as breaking a new record by getting the first perfect score ever awarded for a samba.

'When you go through any season, you want to be memorable,' she says. 'So even though we didn't win, Danny and I will always be in the record books for that samba and that is amazing.

'I am hoping to go as far with Jonnie and I want to get the best out of him and create something that people will always find magical.'

As she embarks on her third *Strictly* series, Oti has one more thing to be excited by: the arrival of a dance idol.

'I'm already a huge fan of Shirley Ballas,' she explains. 'But when I saw her come out dancing, in the beautiful piece of choreography that Jason Gilkison choreographed at the opening of the launch show, I was thinking, "This is why Shirley is one of my idols." She is just amazing and she knows what she's talking about. Her dancing is flawless.'

Oti Mabuse

Claudia Winkleman

Presenter Claudia has been keeping the class of 2017 under a watchful eye as they bond backstage. And this year, she thinks the Clauditorium will be ringing with laughter.

'The contestants are adorable,' she says. 'The line-up is full of real characters so I can't wait to get to know them better. Susan Calman might just be coming home with me – I might have to put her in my pocket because she's wonderful – and I love the Reverend Richard Coles. Brian Conley is hilarious, and Ruth Langsford is already looking after everybody brilliantly. Jonnie is funny and sweet and it's fantastic to have a Paralympian on board. They seem like a really happy and fantastic group.

'They are really gelling and encouraging each other and the camaraderie is strong already. The thing that makes a great *Strictly* is when they all support each other and they had that last year, but I think it's going to happen this year as well.'

While she's summed up their personalities, Claudia admits she hasn't had a chance to assess their prowess on the dance floor, and has no idea who she would tip for the top.

'We saw the group dance on the launch show but I get so over-excited I can't really focus on one person,' she admits. 'There were a few who seemed to have good moves, Gemma looked good, Mollie looked good. But no one messed up the steps and everybody was excellent.'

Claudia has been involved in *Strictly* since 2004, when she began fronting *It Takes Two*, and this will be her fourth year presenting the live shows. But that doesn't stop her brimming with anticipation every September.

'I just can't wait to see them all dance,' she gushes. 'The contestants are brand new, and they'll be nervous, so it's our job to make sure they have a great time.

'I particularly love an Argentine tango, which normally happens later, but when I get my script and it says "A. tango", I'm a profoundly happy girl.'

While Claudia admits she will miss Len Goodman this year, she is thrilled to be welcoming new head judge Shirley Ballas into the fold.

'Shirley is my absolute crush,' she jokes. 'She's fantastic, she's funny and she has the most brilliant laugh. I think she's going to be quite strict. She's a world champion, but she's also taught and judged and there is nothing she hasn't seen, so I think they will really pull out all the stops to impress her. The judges feel like an excellent four and she slots in very well.'

Although Claudia acknowledges that last year's final will be a tough act to follow, she's looking forward to seeing which celebrities shine this year. 'Ore had never danced before, ever, so it shows that you don't have to have previous training to do well, and that's what is so exciting.'

Putting on
THE RITZ

When *Strictly* goes to the pictures on Movie Night, the silver screen comes alive on the dance floor. For costume designer Vicky Gill that means treading a fine line between inspiration and imitation.

'On theme weeks, we are often working with references so we don't want to do a carbon copy,' she explains. 'That rarely works with the dance anyway, because the person who is wearing the dress might want more movement from it, so we shape it to fit the dance. Ultimately it's all about our celebrities and professionals feeling like they can perform live on a Saturday night.'

The more extreme looks, such as *The Mask* outfit worn by Ed Balls, also mean heavy make-up and that can play havoc with the outfits.

'When we are going from dress run into live, when they have full make-up on and they're sweating, they get marks all over the costumes,' says Vicky. 'We often have to strip it all down and get it looking pristine for the live show.'

With a tight schedule for each week's wardrobe, Vicky doesn't always have time to watch all the films featured so she prioritises the ones she doesn't know well.

'If you remember a film already, the viewer will probably have retained all the key information you have and what we want is that immediate acknowledgement, so that they say "Yes, I understand what they did." On the other hand, it's sometimes nice to watch them back because I pick up some quirky details I can slot in that nobody else would know about, but it makes me happy!'

Here's Vicky's pick of the pictures from series 14's Movie Week.

FUN

Ed Balls and Katya Jones

Ed's samba, inspired by Jim Carrey's famous dance in *The Mask*, was definitely smokin' and his bright yellow suit made quite an impact too.

Vicky says: 'Ed was great fun, embracing the whole essence of *Strictly* with a fearless mentality towards anything he was asked to do. He gave it his all on every level.

'For this, we used the film as a reference and the viewer understands the narrative. I don't think there was much doubt on this one!

'The yellow suit worked a treat on screen, but if you were to take a closer look it had more darts and gussets than you could shake a stick at. We really chopped it up to make it fit and work the way we needed it to. If we just bought a yellow suit, it wouldn't stay put, it wouldn't fit under the arms like it needs to, so lots of customising is required and it's like three suits in one. Luckily, the fluorescent colour defused all the lines on screen.

'My assistant Esra always has lots of fun with these numbers – she always pushes boundaries on dress-up weeks.

'Ed was stitched into his costumes close to the show every week, making sure everything was anchored down. While he has an impressive torso, I'm not sure he would want to flash it to the nation on a weekly basis.

'He was slightly superstitious when it came to the weekly dressing routine. Theresa, from dress designer DSI who help out behind the scenes, was the one to do the final stitch, and he poo-pooed any other dressers if she wasn't there. Jane, our wonderful wardrobe supervisor, was always hot on his heels to get him on set.

'Katya is a wonderful clothes horse, full of fun and happy to enter into the spirit of the show. Her dress was in peppermint and simple in design so as not to take the limelight away from Ed. The heavy fringes on the dress worked to create lots of movement.'

ON POINT FOR PERFORMANCE

Ore Oduba and Joanne Clifton

Ore's American smooth, to *Singin' in the Rain*, got rave reviews from the judges – and it scored highly in the style stakes too. Ore looked dapper in a navy pinstripe suit while Jo provided a ray of sunshine with her bright yellow ballroom dress.

Vicky says: 'The cut of the suit is very important for the dancer, cutting high up into the armpit while trying to achieve a smooth top line across the shoulder. The double-breasted, double vent worked a treat, and the wide lapel gave the look of the film. Ore felt the part and ready to perform, which is high on our priority list when working with the celebrities, particularly in the early weeks.

'Jo's base dress was typical of a standard ballroom dress with all the requirements for her American smooth performance. We created a satin wrap-over coat as a nod to the film.

'I was happy for it to have no embellishment, as the colour was doing all the work, but some embellishment was added to the collar as a *Strictly* signature.

'*Strictly* wouldn't be *Strictly* without the sparkle.'

GLAMOUR
Laura Whitmore and Giovanni Pernice

The couple took a trip back to the smoky clubs of *Moulin Rouge* for their lively salsa, with Laura shaking her tail feather in a stunning dress of shimmering silver.

Vicky says: 'This was a real showgirl moment.'

'Laura's dress had a heavily embellished body using approximately 8,000 gold, silver and peach crystals.

A peach boa was added to a removable belt as a reference to the film, giving a long luxurious feel for the moment Laura descended from the rafters on the swing. When it was whipped off, it revealed a smaller version of the tail feather, which allowed Laura to cope with all the movements of her intricate salsa.

'In a previous life, this body was worn by a top-ranking professional Latin dancer called Melia. I customised the shape with embellished hip pads and a beaded skirt for Laura to suit the concept and the *Strictly* setting.

'Giovanni wore a classic black-and-white period suit with a stretch element to suit the needs of the lively performance.'

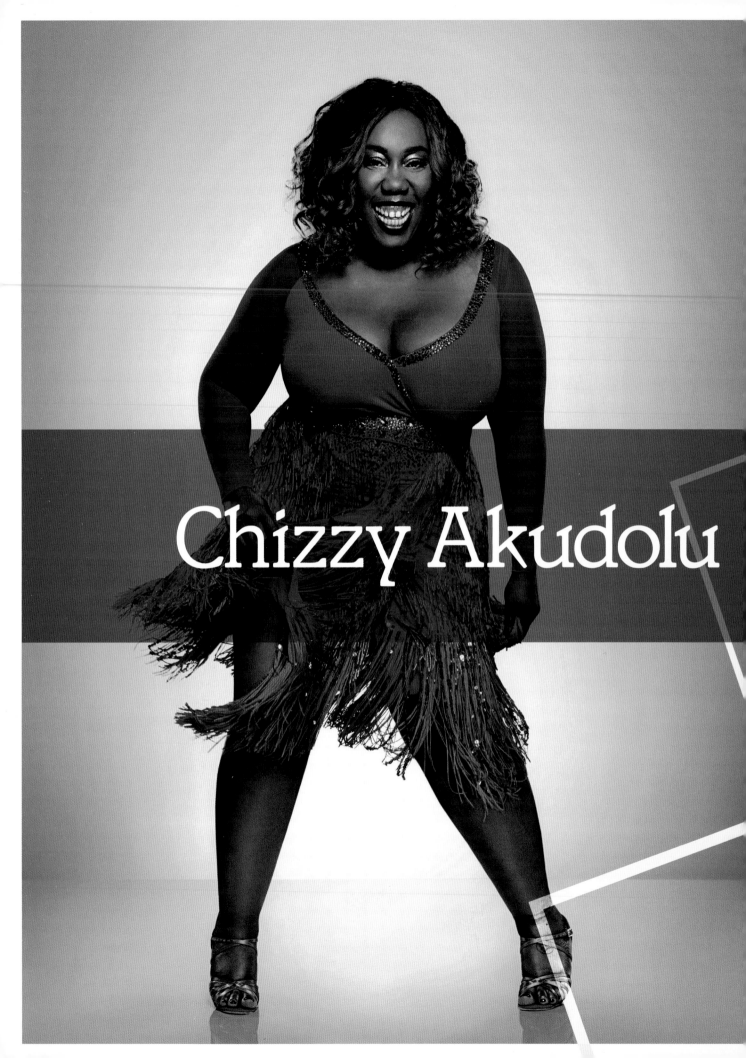

Chizzy Akudolu

Former *Holby City* star Chizzy is looking forward to being 'Strictlified' for the show and says she loves the 'glitz and glamour' of the costumes.

'Everything is beautiful, everything is wonderful, and it's amazing getting glammed up,' she says. '*Strictly* is just one of the most beautiful shows, there is nothing like it on British TV. It's fun, it's a lot of hard work, but it's just gorgeous.'

Born in London in 1973, Chizzy started her showbiz career as a comedy actress, becoming one of eight new comedy performers who won the BBC Talent Initiative, *The Urban Sketch Showcase*, in 2002. She went on to appear in the sitcoms *15 Storeys High* and *Green Wing* as well as the CBBC shows *Stupid!* and *Roman's Empire*. In 2012 she became a permanent fixture on the *Holby City* wards, playing surgeon Mo Effanga for five years, before leaving this summer.

Although Chizzy came second on the 2017 charity show *Let's Sing And Dance For Comic Relief*, performing *Uptown Funk* with two of her co-stars, she says she is a dance novice.

'I have no previous experience, although I did win a disco-dancing competition when I was 13,' she says. 'I can dance, I've got rhythm and I think I can take choreography quite well, but I think it's just going to be the memory and it's all new. Putting your head this way and doing that step, it's going to be tricky.'

Chizzy, who is a brown belt in karate, is looking forward to learning under former champ Pasha Kovalev's tutelage.

'It is amazing to come on the show and learn to dance, being taught by the best people in the world,' she says. 'I'm going to learn to dance, get fit and have a ball, so I couldn't say no.'

She is particularly keen to show her 'fierce' face on the dance floor.

'I can't wait for the Argentine tango because I love the drama of it,' she reveals. 'Also the paso doble, because I love all that cape work and the intense expressions. It's so dramatic.'

The actress is up against her former *Holby* colleague Joe McFadden, but she couldn't be happier.

'It's really nice to have somebody that I know taking part as well,' she says. 'I thought if anyone was horrible at least I would have a friendly face but everyone is lovely. As for any rivalry, it's friendly.'

Siberian dancer Pasha joined *Strictly* in series 9, and he's looking forward to getting back into the ballroom for his seventh series.

This year Pasha is paired up with *Holby City* actress Chizzy Akudolu, and thinks she is scrubbing up well on the dance floor.

'We're getting the dance down and she's doing great,' he says. 'She's very funny, so we are having fun, but I know that she is ready to give everything, all the energy she has, all the dedication she has, all the time she has, to improve her dancing, and that's the best thing ever.

'I think she will be feeling the Latin vibe. She likes all that hip action and quick rhythm. She is definitely a party girl.'

Although she has no dance experience, Pasha believes Chizzy's acting skills will come to the fore in her routines.

'Chizzy is a lot of fun, she's a good actress and she brings a lot of personality to the dance floor,' he says. 'Dance is a combination of things. You have to have technique, you have to have energy, and you have to have characterisation and chemistry with your partner.'

Pasha began dancing at the age of eight and, after winning amateur Latin championships in Russia with dance partner Anya Garnis, moved to the US in 2001. Last year, he was partnered with Naga Munchetty, who was the third celebrity eliminated.

'Naga was fun and she was also determined to get better,' says Pasha. 'She loved learning and she loved dancing. I felt we left the competition just at the moment she was beginning to really feel the dance, so I wish we had had another week… or six.'

While Pasha is passionate about his routines, he doesn't mind the comments from the judges.

'The judges only say things to make you better. They want you to improve certain aspects of your dance so that hopefully you get to the next level by the following week.'

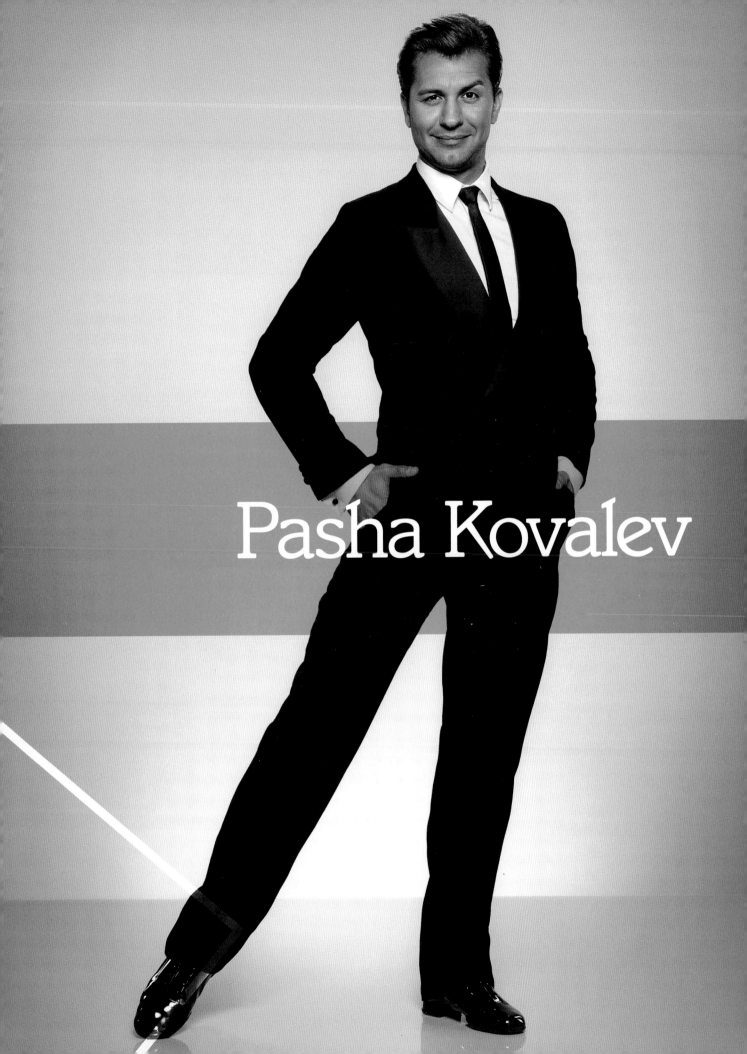

Pasha Kovalev

Darcey Bussell

Our former prima ballerina is back to keep all the celebrities on their toes and as a relative newcomer to the panel – having joined permanently in 2012 – she was also on hand to support new head judge Shirley Ballas at the launch show.

'Before going on I was holding her hand and saying, "I know what you're feeling. Don't worry",' reveals Darcey. 'But she had no problems at all and she kept her calm amid all the excitement. She knows dance inside out and she's a brilliant addition to the team.'

The pair are already planning to trade tips. 'I'm going to see her judge at the Albert Hall and she's going to come and watch me coach with the Royal Ballet Company,' says Darcey. 'So we're showing each other what we do.'

What do you make of the line-up?

It's a really interesting mix. They are great characters and from contrasting backgrounds, but there are a few 'show people' so that will make the performance side quite exciting, which I always enjoy, because I can see their personality.

What did you think of the pairings when they were announced?

I love the pairing of Debbie and Giovanni. Also, Reverend Richard and Dianne, because she's a fireball Australian and I think she'll push him really hard. It's tough for the new dancers, stepping in straight away, but I think they will be great. Chizzy with Pasha will be divine. She's very funny but nothing is going to stop her.

Jonnie Peacock could be fantastic. What a role model for anybody who lives with a disability. His pairing with Oti is inspired, because she won't let it hold her back either and I think he'll be ready to try anything. I'm expecting impressive stuff from Aston and Janette too.

What did you make of the Bruce Forsyth tribute on the launch show?

It was very moving and the dance was beautiful. Those dancers all seemed to have a bit of Bruce in them. Bruce was such an icon. I don't believe he'll ever really be gone from this show because there is such a permanent image of him, next to the band and being the ultimate entertainer.

What are you looking forward to most this year?

I'm always struck with the staging and hard work that goes into the themed weekends, so I always get excited about those, and I love December. We get to do the Christmas show, which I enjoy because I love the festive period, and when it builds to those last three shows of the series, it's an exciting time. But there are so many fabulous things about *Strictly* and I always feel incredibly privileged to be part of it.

Simon Rimmer

Celebrity chef Simon is hoping he'll be cooking with gas on the dance floor after taking the lead from guests on his *Sunday Brunch* show.

'We have had so many *Strictly* contestants on over the years and every single one has said that it is simply the greatest experience they've ever had,' he says. 'So when I was asked to take part, it literally took me a split second to say "yes", even though it's a terrifying prospect.'

Simon was born in Merseyside in 1963 and taught himself to cook after studying for a career in fashion and textiles. He opened his first restaurant, Greens, in Manchester at the age of 27, and followed up with a second, Earle, in 2006. After guest appearances on several shows, including *This Morning*, he teamed up with Tim Lovejoy in 2006. Their Sunday morning BBC2 show, *Something for the Weekend*, launched a screen partnership that lasts to this day, and the pair have fronted Channel 4's *Sunday Brunch* since 2012. The banter between the two has led to a huge fan following and Simon admits he is getting 'plenty of stick' from his co-host over his dancing ability.

'Tim is just as supportive as you'd imagine him to be,' he laughs. 'My favourite quote so far is, "I'm going to come to the first show because I want to make sure that I get to see you once."'

Although he has no dance experience, the dad of two thinks his competitive nature and love of learning will prove the right recipe to spice up the dance floor.

'I have genuinely never danced before so the first day of rehearsals was the first day I had ever danced, and that was quite scary.

'One of the big moments for me was the first time I watched the pro-dancers dance without us lumbering about with them. You have a couple of days of practising the group dance and you think, "Yes, I'm starting to get this", and then you watch the pros dance and you think, "Oh my word! We have no idea what we're doing."

'But I am loving it and it's hard not to. Every single second that you are involved in it is so positive. I just want to learn and be competitive and be much better than I am.'

While he's keen to up his own dance-floor game, Simon has also been keeping an eye on the competition in the run-up to the live shows. 'Aston is brilliant, Alexandra is good, and Debbie McGee looks great, so poised.

'In fact, I can probably list 14 people who are my main competition.'

Unlike many of his fellow competitors, Simon will have no chance for a lie-in after dancing the night away on Saturday's live shows.

'I'm on the studio at 6am on Sunday morning so I will have to go from Elstree to Central London after the show and get up at 5.30am and do three hours of *Sunday Brunch*. It's going to be a challenge but I'm looking forward to it.'

As something of a foodie, Karen was over the moon to be paired with *Sunday Brunch* star Simon Rimmer.

'Being paired with Simon came as a surprise,' she reveals. 'I was really happy. We started training on a Sunday because his schedule is manic, so he brought me some food straight from *Sunday Brunch*. He brought me some couscous salad and some big cookies, and it was the one of the best meals I have ever eaten. Every morning he brings me coffee, which is a must, and chocolate as well – good chocolate, not just any chocolate.'

Karen is hoping her new pupil will teach her a thing or two, to improve her culinary skills.

'One of the things I love about *Strictly* is what you learn from your partner, and his talent is cooking, which is one of my favourite things in the whole wide world, so I'm hoping to get as many recipes and cooking tips as possible.'

Originally from Venezuela, Karen moved to New York when she was eight years old, later becoming the United Amateur American Rhythm National Champion and Professional World Mambo Champion. Karen, who is married to fellow *Strictly* pro Kevin, joined the show in series 10 and reached the grand final with Mark Wright in 2014.

Karen says Simon is serving up some tasty footwork already.

'Simon is surprising me,' she says. 'He is working extremely hard. His work ethic is beyond anything I have seen before and when I explain everything fully he gets it, which is really good. He's a complete beginner but at the same time he is very physically fit because he has done boxing and Pilates and he connects really well with his body. I'm not making it easy for him at all but I'm happy with him so far.

'He's doing a lot right now and filming another show so he's trying to put in as many hours as possible but I don't think it's about the quantity of the hours, it's about how much work he puts in. You can train the whole day and not get much done, but he knows he is under pressure to get everything done within a certain time, which means he gives me 100 per cent. And I am definitely a hard taskmaster so I don't waste a minute.'

However well he does in the live shows, there will be no celebrating on Saturday night, as Simon has to be up at the crack of dawn on Sunday for his own live show.

'Hopefully he'll wake up really happy because he's made it through to the next week.'

Karen Clifton

HOLLYWOOD HAIR

For her *Moulin Rouge* routine on Movie Week, Laura Whitmore conjured up the fiery glamour of the film with flowing, flaming locks. To get the look, however, the presenter had to hide her trademark long blonde hair, and go for a total transformation.

Strictly stylist Lisa Davey explains: 'The hair was a real wig and we used a dark red, which we set in a Marcel wave, and to give it more length we added some extra pieces that we coloured to match.

'During the week, we set it on small rollers all in one direction, so that when the rollers came out and we brushed it through, it set into the Marcel wave of the *Moulin Rouge* era.

'However, it was quite hard to keep that up throughout the Saturday of the show because she was rehearsing the dance and moving about a lot. That kind of look is a great aesthetic for the red carpet, but when they are dancing in it you have to work really hard and keep resetting it to make sure it stays looking good throughout the day.

'After we set it and put it on, we added hair jewellery to it, to one side, to complement the theme and the costume. Then we used tons of hairspray to keep it all in place during her energetic salsa.'

While using a wig means the stylists can carry on working on the look without the celebrity being in the room, it also has its pitfalls – namely the possibility of it moving or worse, falling off. But the *Strictly* team have the solution pinned down.

'We prepped Laura's hair before adding the wig,' says Lisa. 'First, we flatten it down as much as we can, then put on a wig cap, which is pinned on. Then, in four spots across the head, we cross over two little clips to make anchor points.

'When we put the wig on, we fix the wig to the head really well with plenty of pins. After that, we go in and, underneath the pins that are already attached to Laura's head, we find the little anchor points and use more pins to attach the wig to those points so it doesn't move. We have to pin it extremely well so that it stays on.

'The salsa is a very lively dance so as the day went on we worked and worked on the wig to the point it was set and it was not going to move. It's a really set look and when they are moving around it can unravel. A couple of strands were coming loose by the end but the rest of it stayed in place, so I was pleased with that.'

LIPSTICK and ROUGE

The Movie Week transformation from *Strictly* contestant to screen icon wouldn't be complete without the magical touch of the make-up department.

In Laura Whitmore's case, Hair and Make-up Designer Lisa Armstrong played her part in conjuring up the mood of *Moulin Rouge* by creating her own take on the iconic showgirl and then handed the reins to make-up artist Lottie Brooksbank.

'The look in the film is the inspiration but Laura's look is our own take on that, tailored to her skin tone, dress colour, etc.,' explains Lottie. 'Lisa came up with the look and then talked me through the costume, told me what she wanted and gave me a mood board with *Moulin Rouge* references.

'When the celebrity is in the chair we also take into account their preferences and anything they would like to change. 'Unless the look is very specific and set, we will always try and accommodate their wishes.'

> '[Lisa] gave me a mood board with *Moulin Rouge* references'

HERE'S HOW LOTTIE ACHIEVED LAURA'S SILVER-SCREEN SALSA LOOK:

Prep 'As always, I prepped the skin and eyes with a cleanser then moisturised the face.'

Eyes 'I started with prep and prime base to conceal any tiny veins on the eyelid and to smooth out the tone. Next, I put a naked eyeshadow all over to make the eye all one colour and neat then I shaded with brown in the socket and against the lash line. Using a black liner I drew a flick on the top lashes. I used loads of mascara on the bottom and top lashes and, as it's *Strictly*, I added false lashes. I chose a pair that was thicker at the ends to help with the flick. After doing the eyes, I always clean up underneath with a wet wipe because eyeshadow often drops down or a dust of mascara might fall, then I reapply a touch of moisturiser there.'

Base 'For the base I used a foundation with good coverage. On *Strictly* you need that, because they are dancing and sweating.'

Cheek 'I bronzed her cheeks to give her some contouring in her cheek socket and used a little peachy blusher and powder shimmer on her cheekbones to make them glow.'

Lips 'I used red lip liner then filled it with a red lipstick. We don't use lip gloss in the Latin dances if someone's hair is down because they flick their head and their hair gets stuck on the lips, which is not a good look.'

Finish 'We finished the face with lots of powder. The costume department then gave me a couple of crystals to match the dress and I stuck them in the inner corner of her eyes with eyelash glue, so they were not in danger of moving anywhere. It was great to add a bit of sparkle as a final touch.'

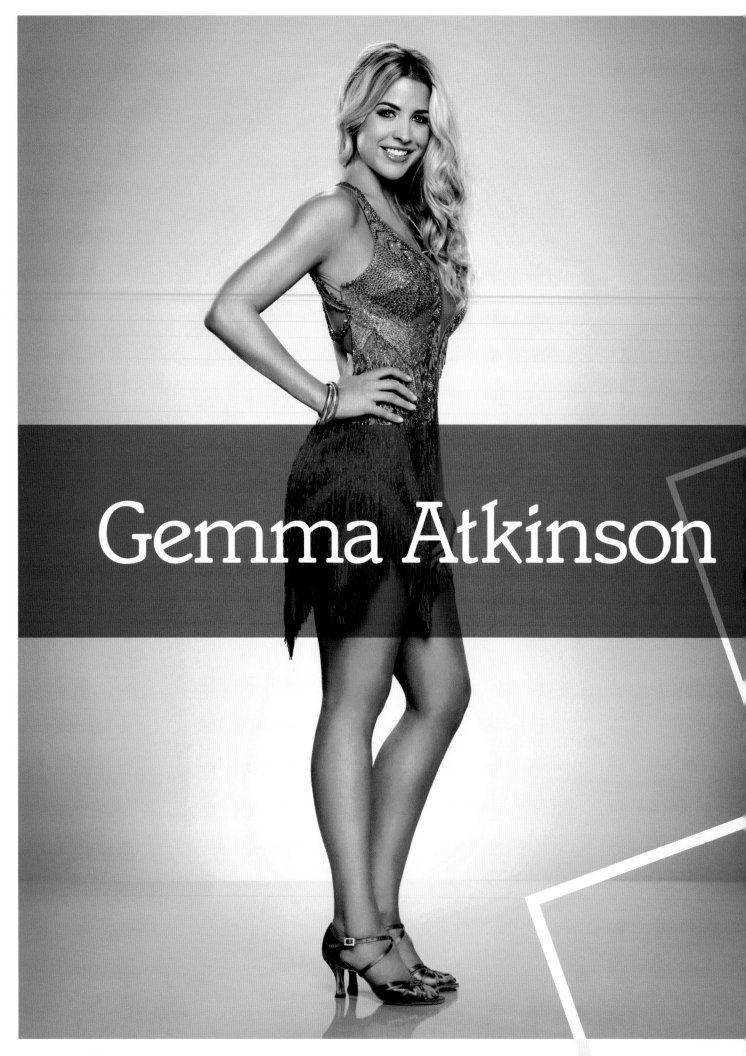

Gemma Atkinson

Soap star Gemma is more comfortable in the gym than on the dance floor, and has hardly ever danced in heels. But it's not messing up the routine on a Saturday night that is her greatest fear – it's what happens next.

'The biggest worry for me is running up the stairs after the dance,' she reveals. 'Because you are high on adrenalin from the dance, the camera is in front of you, the rest of the couples are at the top, so it's almost like a stairway to heaven in that when you get up there you can relax. But you've got to run up them first. I'm not great at running anyway, let alone up the stairs, in heels, after I've been dancing.'

The Mancunian star was born in 1984 and rose to fame as Lisa Hunter in the Channel 4 soap *Hollyoaks*. After five years, and two spin-off series, Gemma headed to *Casualty* before taking on the role of Carly Hope in *Emmerdale* in 2015.

But there was one role her family have always wanted to see her in.

'Every time I get another job and I tell my family, they say, "That's amazing. It would be really good if you could do *Strictly* one day."' She laughs. 'My mum's been on my case for years. So when I told the family I had to swear them to secrecy, but there were a lot of screams.'

Even so, she is considering banning her mum from the studio audience on the live shows – for her own good.

'I don't want my mum there because she will worry for me,' she explains. 'They are going to come down but I know my mum will be nervous for me before I go on and I don't like her stressing for me. It's a mum's job to feel like that, but I want her to be home with a cup of tea and watching it chilled.'

As tomboy Carly, Gemma was more often seen in jeans and dungarees than ballgowns and she admits the *Strictly* costume fittings have been an eye-opener.

'The dresses are gorgeous,' she says. 'The wardrobe team are amazing. They hand-stitch every detail. Their work is just incredible.'

That's not the only surprise for the fitness fanatic, who has discovered muscles she never knew she had.

'I work out a lot and I thought my fitness would put me in good stead to dance but I soon discovered there's a completely different level of fitness required,' she admits. 'I was so achy after the first day of training. It's way out of everybody's comfort zone. We were all messaging saying how much were aching and how surprising it is. I'm more comfortable in a weights room than I am in a frock. But I'm really enjoying the training!'

Former champ Aljaž lifted the glitter ball trophy on his debut year, in 2013, with model Abbey Clancy, and this year he's hoping to get the double with soap actress Gemma Atkinson. Before starting on their first dance, he had already put her through her paces – and was pleased with the results.

'We did the basics of both Latin and ballroom so I could get the feel of what to do with the choreography, and the difficulty of steps, and so far she has coped really well,' he reveals. 'She has loads of potential. She is very fit because she works out and she's very active in her normal life, so she is taking the rehearsals in the same way and giving it her all. She is used to training her body, although dancing is completely different, but it means she has a lot of stamina. In fact, I think she might have more stamina than me!

'Gemma is really good fun. She is a swift learner, she is really keen and hard-working. I think it's going to be a lovely season for me.'

Born in Slovenia, Aljaž started dancing at the age of five and has enjoyed success in his home country, where he won the national championships 19 times. For over a decade, Aljaž represented Slovenia in the World Latin and Ballroom Championships. After winning his first *Strictly* trophy with Abbey, he has been partnered by Alison Hammond, Helen George and, last year, by Daisy Lowe.

'I have been so lucky with all my celebrity partners,' he says. 'They have all been lovely and Daisy was the same. We had a great time. I think she could have stayed in the competition longer but it was a very tough year, there was a lot of great talent.

'There are some numbers with Daisy that I'm going to be proud of for ever. For example, the week 1 waltz that was dedicated to her late grandpa was a very special moment for her. She was just a lovely girl and we became good friends. We're still in touch today.'

In fact, Daisy was a guest at Aljaž's wedding to Janette Manrara earlier this summer.

'The wedding was stunning,' he recalls. 'It was really nice to celebrate together with friends.'

Aljaž Škorjanec

Zoe Ball

As soon as she stepped into her own dancing shoes as a series 3 competitor, Zoe Ball was hooked. So when she was asked to present *It Takes Two* in 2011, she didn't have to think twice.

'I feel blessed because once you have done the show you become a complete superfan,' she admits. 'We think we're all armchair experts, even though we're probably not, so *It Takes Two* is the best job in the world for me.'

Although she and partner Ian Waite finished third, she fell in love with the whole experience. Now every year Zoe waltzes back into the *Strictly* bubble and becomes just a little bit obsessed.

'I move into the studio,' she laughs. 'We have beds under the stairs! There's no point in talking to me about anything other than *Strictly* for three months. I get genuinely excited.

'It's so much fun to work with Ian and designer Vicky Gill and we are like an extended family. We love getting together for a chat about all things *Strictly*.'

As well as getting to meet the competing couples, Zoe loves the 'Friday panel' with celebrity superfans, including Michael Ball, Alexander Armstrong and Jeremy Vine.

'I love seeing grown people discussing their favourites and whether something was a proper rumba,' she laughs. 'I've also got to know a lot of the dancers and I love that I get to share their *Strictly* experience with the audience.

'I love that we are on for half an hour in the

week and people say it's a family tradition to have their tea and then sit down for *It Takes Two*. In the autumn months, when the weather gets colder, we're a little shot of sparkle every day.'

Although no longer required to train on a daily basis, Zoe still likes a twirl.

'One of the best things is that I still get to have a little swing round with my partner Ian. You never forget the moves. I can't do them the way I did on the show, but occasionally in the bathroom, if something comes on I'll think, "This is a samba beat" and I'll pull off a little botafogo.'

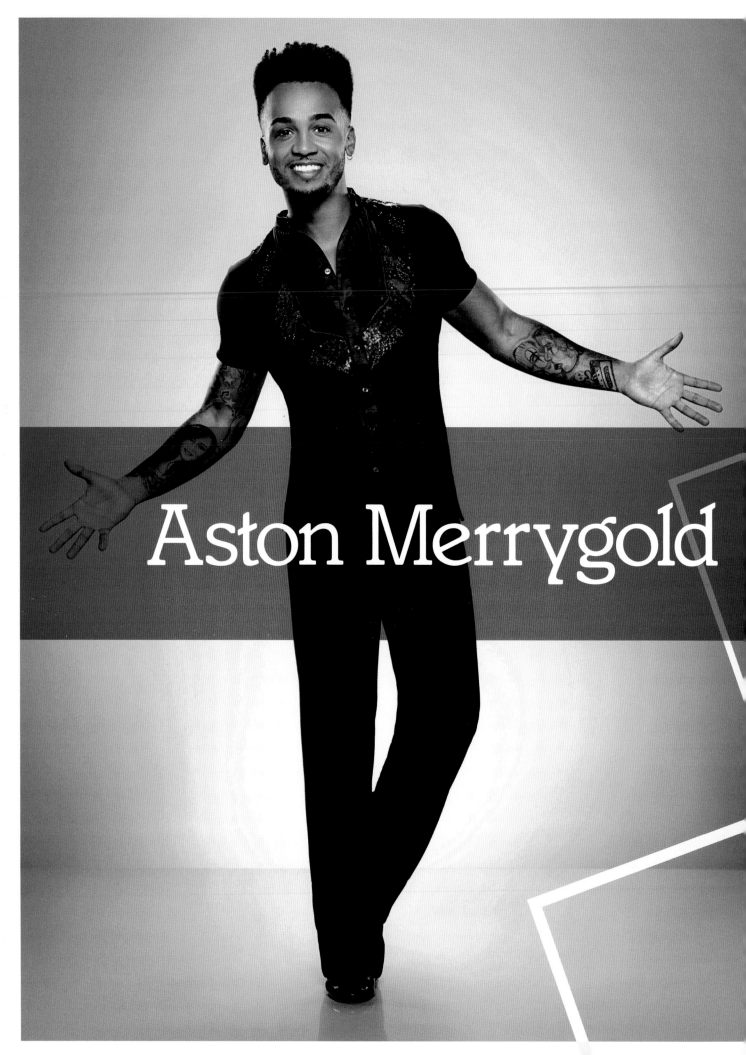

Aston Merrygold

Aston shot to fame on *The X Factor* when his boy band, JLS, reached the final. And he'll have a familiar face in the *Strictly* ballroom with fellow *X Factor* finalist Alexandra Burke.

We make a joke of it, talking about round two, but what's special about this show and why people are so eager to sign up for it, is that off-screen everyone has such a good time together,' he explains. 'And as much as it is a competition, it really isn't because we all get on so well and that's the nicest thing. None of us want to leave but at the same time we don't want anyone else to leave. So you're really in competition with yourself.'

Born in 1988, Aston was raised in Northern Ireland and made his first TV appearance at 14, impersonating Michael Jackson on *Stars in Their Eyes*. Shortly after leaving school, he was chosen to front a children's show *Fun Song Factory*, before being asked to audition for a new boy band by friend Marvin Humes. The success of JLS on *The X Factor* propelled them to global fame and a string of number one hits, including *One Shot*, *Everybody in Love* and *Love You More*.

Despite his experience of performing in a band, Aston insists he is a real beginner when it comes to a waltz or a foxtrot.

'I've never done ballroom before,' he says. 'People probably expect me to be good because of the performance aspect, and obviously I have performed in front of crowds, but in terms of ballroom and Latin, there was never an opportunity to learn that. Me and the boys were never in hold! When one of the professional dancers put me in hold the other day, I had no idea what I was doing. It's a completely different discipline.'

Aston was at a family wedding when the news that he had signed up for *Strictly* surfaced – and it caused much excitement.

'I have a couple of great-aunts and my nan who are full-on fans, and throw *Strictly* parties every year,' he says. 'When the news broke, I was at a wedding with them and they kept saying, "Is it true?" Every time I turned round my aunt was there, trying to find out.

While he has his eye firmly on the glitter ball, Aston insists his real goal is just to make it through to the end.

'Winning is great, but to reach the final, and live the whole *Strictly* experience, that's the goal. To learn a whole new dance each week, and do Halloween and Blackpool, and all of those things will be enough.

'There aren't many shows out there that allow you to learn a brand-new skill and that are so relaxed at the same time. I thought there would be more pressure, but everybody is so lovely and chilled so it's even better than I was hoping and it's a lovely opportunity.'

At five foot, Janette is the smallest of the pro dancers and that's one of the reasons she had her eye on Aston Merrygold as soon as the new line-up was announced.

'I was crossing all my fingers that I got him because I got on well with him in rehearsals and we became good friends really quickly,' she reveals. 'He's also the perfect height for me! It's nice to have someone who is a great person, talented, and the right height, all in one so I was really over the moon.'

As part of hit group JLS, Aston was famed for his acrobatic moves, and while Janette says she's 'not giving too much away', she hints that viewers may be seeing some impressive tricks in her routines. But she says his pop background is not making the training any easier.

'He's never done ballroom or Latin so he is going through the same paces as everyone else, in that he has to do it over and over again and it is taking him a little bit of time to understand how it's meant to feel and look,' she says. 'He was self-taught so he's never been in a dance class before, so he's finding it a little bit hard. But he works so hard and I'm really excited for what I hope will be an awesome series.'

Born in Miami, Janette was a principal dancer in the TV series and live tour of *Glee*. She was also a finalist in season five of the US show *So You Think You Can Dance*. She joined *Strictly* in 2013 and, although she was first to leave with Melvin Odoom last year, they went on to win the *Strictly Come Dancing* Christmas Special together.

'I felt gutted for Melvin that his journey got cut short, and he is such a nice guy so I wanted him to have a bit more of the *Strictly* experience,' she says. 'When we got invited to do the Christmas special, we were just happy to be dancing together again, but the icing on the cake was that we also won it, so it was a perfect way to end 2016. We were both so happy.'

This year has also proved an eventful one for Janette, who tied the knot with fellow pro Aljaž Škorjanec in July.

'It was incredible, it was the best day of my life,' she says.

Janette Manrara

STEPS to SUCCESS

If you fancy giving the Fearsome Foursome a run for their money and becoming an armchair judge, you'll need to know your rise and fall from your heel and toe leads. Who better to give us a quick dance lesson than former *Strictly* pros Karen Hardy and Ian Waite? Here are their tips on what the judges are looking for on some of the key *Strictly* dances.

WALTZ

Karen says:

'The waltz is one of our oldest dances, dating back to the 17th century. This means it's not just the judges on the panel you have to please, but the millions of judges watching at home, who will also have some experience of the dance – and there will be clear things that they will be

'The technical element is the beautiful rise and fall in this dance and that comes from the footwork. One of my little sayings is "footwork is the foundation of movement". From early on, the celebrity needs to master the heels and toes and that will create the rise and fall to impress the judges.

'The second tip is to get the top line as soon as possible. The elbows should be kept in front of the body and never pulled behind. The aim is to use your legs for movement and your body for changing direction, and not to use your arms. You are also looking for full body contact.

'Each dance has a very strong character to master and this dance has grace, romance, elegance and flow. It can't have a 1, 2, 3 stop… everything has to have a beautiful flow.

'Finally, you have the musicality, so the basic rhythm is 1, 2, 3 and we always accent the one. The waltz is a progressive dance – which means it moves round the floor – so you want

must keep that energy from beginning to end. Sometimes it will be programmed into the routine that there will be more energetic parts than others, so you will have the time to rest and breathe in between, but you need to make sure that when you get to the energetic parts, you give it your everything. The jive is all about maintaining and giving out energy throughout the whole dance.

'When it comes to the connection between the two dancers, when you are in hold, make sure it's nice and short because then you can stay connected to each other and you can keep your body weight towards each other.'

JIVE

Ian says:

'There's a particular stance in jive, which is pulled up in the tummy and almost like you are lifted from your behind, so you feel as if you are stooping over straight legs. You need to stay up on the balls of your feet and your knees have to come almost up to your chest.

'There are a lot of flicks and kicks in jive, so you pick up your knee and the back heel almost touches the backside before you flick your toe.

'Keep the kicks and flicks nice and neat so that you can create the speed and the accuracy that you need. While you are keeping it precise, keep your muscles loose, then you can retract them and flick them really quickly. If you try to flex the muscles, it slows you down because you are holding the muscles when you need to release them and flick the feet with a loose movement.

'The jive has got tremendous energy, so you

PASO DOBLE

Karen says:

'This most Spanish of dances actually originated as a party dance among aristocrats in Paris and over many years it has changed to become the dramatic, dominant story of the matador in the bull ring.

'Understanding the characterisation is very demanding, but it requires dominance from both partners. The underlying theme is intense love and passion at the highest level so that it creates this energy of aggression and assertiveness, the ultimate love/hate relationship on the dance floor.

'From the male, we are looking for the strong matador with beautiful, long, curving shapes, created from the feet, up through the body and right up to the tips of the fingers. There can be no part of the shape left out.

'For the lady, mastering shapes is also important, and she can be both submissive and assertive, with the beautiful tension through the body. This is the one Latin dance where the celebrity needs to master heel leads, which will then move the body with assertiveness and tension rather than grace.

'The judges look for shaping and characterisation, and this can only be achieved by understanding the technical elements of heel leads.

'The legs are straight not locked, the pelvis is towards the front of the feet, and the ribcage is held very high with the shoulders relaxed over the top.'

FOXTROT

Ian says:

'The foxtrot is like the Rolls-Royce of dances. Smooth gliding steps, with long flowing movements.

'The lady must reach back with her toe to give the man a chance to stride out. The tip is to hold the slows as long as possible.

'The hold is a traditional ballroom hold and you want to create as much "flower in a vase", as I always say, as you can. What that means is that you are creating the roundness at the top of the hold, which is the opening of the vase, the slimness of the vase is where the two bodies connect together and the lady's head is like a flower stretching out of the vase.'

CHA-CHA-CHA

Ian says:

'The cha-cha is a cheeky, fun flirty dance and it has a sharp, compact leg action so you need snappy straight legs.

'There's a constant hip action which flows from side to side, and as you settle into the hip, your shoulder blades should settle into the movement.

'Keep your steps small, and this will help you straighten your legs at speed.'

SAMBA

Karen says:

'The samba is the hardest of the Latin dances because it has 11 different rhythms. Some make the dancer bounce on the dance floor, some are flat, and some make it look like you hover across the floor.

'For a great samba you need brilliant choreography, and by choosing the right steps you can use all the rhythms. For example, there's the plait, which is flat, and the promenade runs, which have a hovering effect. The challenge is for the celebrity to grasp the rhythms and this comes down to understanding footwork.

'In the Latin dances, we use toe leads 99 per cent of the time and heel leads are rare. A soft knee is key throughout, so a technical term would be "straight not locked".

'The samba is a flamboyant festival of a dance, so it's really conjuring up that essence of fun, vibrancy, colour and a Rio carnival vibe. Not over-concentrating but bringing the audience into your performance is essential in this dance.

'Even though you are having a party, remember there are two of you moving around the dance floor and that will go a long way in creating the image of teamwork.'

Susan Calman

As a topical comedian, Susan likes to put a smile on her audience's faces – and that's precisely why she signed up for *Strictly Come Dancing*.

'I love the show,' she explains. 'The news is all doom and gloom so it's no wonder people like to turn on the telly and watch people doing a Charleston. For an hour and a half, we are watching people have a nice time on a great show.

'It's the same reason I went into comedy. I want people to be happier when they leave my show than when they arrive, and *Strictly* does that. It really is a ray of sunshine.'

Susan grew up in Glasgow and studied law at Glasgow University before embarking on a successful legal career. After seven years, she swapped the courtroom for the comedy clubs and, in 2005, was a semi-finalist in the BBC New Comedy Awards before winning Best New Scottish Comedian at the Real Radio Variety Awards in 2009. Since then, she has become a regular voice on Radio 4, guesting on *The News Quiz* and *I'm Sorry I Haven't a Clue*, as well as starring in her own radio sitcom *Sisters* and two series of her stand-up show *Susan Calman is Convicted*. She also fronts the CBBC show *Top Class* and the BBC1 show *The Boss*.

The Scottish comic remembers some ceilidh classes at school but has no other dance experience. She has already managed to exceed even her own expectations.

'If I can do *Strictly* as a 42-year-old who has never danced and never worn a dress, anyone can do it,' she says. 'I'm surprised that I'm not awful. I am surprised I have worn a dress. It really is the show that can make anything happen.

'Also, I wasn't expecting to feel such pride in my fellow competitors. We haven't known each other long but they sent us a wee video of our rehearsal of the opening number, to help us remember it, and I was watching it and saying, "Oh, they did that brilliantly."'

Being vocal and opinionated may be essential for her panel shows and comic routines, but Susan insists the Fearsome Foursome won't be getting a tongue-lashing from her.

'It's a competition so you are going to have people judging you and if you don't want to be judged, you're in the wrong show,' she reasons. 'Secondly, it's part of the entertainment, and Craig Revel Horwood judging you is part of the joy of *Strictly*.

'I'm taking a leaf out of Jeremy Vine's book because every time he had low scores from Craig, he just went, "Ha, you're right." I think that's the best way to do it. Actually, Craig is a lovely fellow. If he wants to pass comment on my dancing, I will take it as a badge of honour.'

Grimsby lad Kevin may not have bagged the glitter ball but he has broken a record – as the only professional dancer to make four consecutive finals.

'It's becoming a running theme now, making the final and then being a runner-up,' he laughs. 'That's four years in a row!'

Kevin was born into a dancing family and taught by his parents, former World Champions Keith and Judy Clifton, going on to win International Open titles all over the world. He is a former Youth World Number One and four-time British Latin Champion and has starred in the West End.

Since joining *Strictly* in 2013 he reached the final with Susanna Reid, Frankie Bridge, Kellie Bright and, last year, with Louise Redknapp.

'Louise was one of the sweetest people I've ever met,' he says. 'On week 1, she said, "Please don't expect too much of me." She really wanted to do it, so to watch how she grew and blossomed throughout the competition was amazing. From about halfway through she started to really enjoy it and come out of herself and by the end I thought she was magnificent. I was so proud of her and how far she came.'

This year Kevin is partnered with superfan Susan Calman, who admitted on the launch show that she had a picture of him on her fridge.

'It's good to feel appreciated,' laughs Kevin. 'Susan and her wife are both massive *Strictly* fans who have been watching it for years so they are really interested and asking me loads of questions, but it's great fun.'

In order to train with Susan, Kevin is spending most of his time in her hometown of Glasgow, and says his latest pupil is throwing herself into training.

'She's a hard worker,' he says. 'She's putting a lot of effort in and she understands what I'm saying and applies it straight away. She's also relentless. For our first Viennese waltz she was getting a bit dizzy and felt a bit sick after the spins, but she won't stop and never wants a break. She's really excited about the whole thing.

'The most important thing to me is getting a partner you get on with and have a laugh with, so it doesn't get overly serious in the training room. Susan's really funny and we're having a great time.'

Kevin Clifton

Davood Ghadami

EastEnders star Davood joins a long line of actors who have waltzed their way from Albert Square to the *Strictly* ballroom, following in the well-placed footsteps of Scott Maslen, Jake Wood and Tameka Empson. Now his co-stars are rallying round to give him support.

'Tameka, Jake and Scott are so excited on my behalf,' he reveals, 'Seeing their excitement when I could finally tell them brought it all home to me and I realised I was going to have so much fun in this show. They were all blown away when they did it and they've been giving me some great little tips.

'Their faces lit up when they were talking about it and that's how I know that when I look back on this experience it will all be really positive. I'm trying to soak up every moment of it.'

Davood was born in Harlow in 1982 and has starred in *Taggart* as regular Duncan Clark, as well as appearing in *Doctor Who*, *Spooks* and *Law & Order*. His films include *John Carter* and *Red Mercury*. In 2014, the actor joined the cast of *EastEnders* as market trader Kush Kazemi for which he won Best Newcomer at the TV Choice Awards.

With no dance experience, Davood signed up to *Strictly* because he is keen to learn a new skill.

'I'm not a natural dancer, no way, and I wouldn't choose to go out and dance,' he admits. 'For me this is a blank canvas, a start, and it's nice when things like that come up in life. If an opportunity comes along I will take it.

'I am really enjoying meeting new people, seeing how great the professional dancers are, and becoming part of that whole process. If I can come out of the end of every week saying to myself, "Actually, I just did a waltz" or "I did a foxtrot" – that's what I'm looking forward to. That's the ultimate aim.'

Davood, who will be splitting his time between the *EastEnders* set and the training room during his run, says he is definitely up for a good time.

'If you're enjoying what you're doing I think that translates into the dance,' he says. 'The tricky bit is going to be leading someone who has taught you to lead, but hopefully each dance will be practised so many times that I can lead, but if I need help, my partner Nadiya will be there to pull me along.'

He's hoping he will learn enough to show off his moves at future social occasions.

'Everyone will be watching us, at every event,' he says. 'Once we've done *Strictly* everyone will be saying, "Go on then, show us what you've got".'

Ukrainian dancer Nadiya has come straight from the world of competitive dancing to join the *Strictly* family and is enjoying each new challenge the show brings.

'I am so happy to be joining the show,' she says. 'It will be a really amazing experience so I am looking forward to the whole series.

'Everything that is happening is very special. My *Strictly* journey started with a whole month of rehearsals with the pro dancers, which is great experience for me, because I come from a competitive world and it's a nice feeling to create something beautiful with all of the team and to feel like I'm part of something really big.

'Then after a month of group rehearsals I got my celebrity partner so I'm really happy.'

Born in Ukraine, Nadiya took up dancing at the age of five – which is not as early as she would have liked.

'I had seen some dance performances and I really wanted to do it when I was four but the dance school said I was too young,' she reveals. 'So I was waiting for a whole year and then when I was five I still wanted to do it, so I went back. I've been dancing ever since.'

She is now two-time World Champion and European Champion in ballroom and Latin '10' Dance and has multiple national ballroom and Latin Champion titles under her belt.

Although it's her first year, Nadiya has high hopes for her soap-actor partner, *EastEnders* star Davood Ghadami.

'I think he has got good potential,' she says. 'It's not easy for a non-dancer because he hasn't done any kind of dancing ever, so he's learning from the very beginning, but he is picking things up quickly. It takes time to learn how to move the body, to put the muscles and the bones in the right position, but we are working on it.

'We are working on his hips for the first Latin dance, as I know that is what the judges will be looking for.'

As well as making a move on to the *Strictly* dance floor, Nadiya has had to pack up and move to the UK, with the blessing of her family.

'My family were very supportive,' she says. 'They know I love doing what I'm doing and they think it's a great opportunity for me.

'I have been to the UK lots of times because of my dance career and dance competitions. I really like it here because it has some history for me from when I was really little, coming here to Blackpool for the British Opens and all the big competitions, so I am happy to be here.'

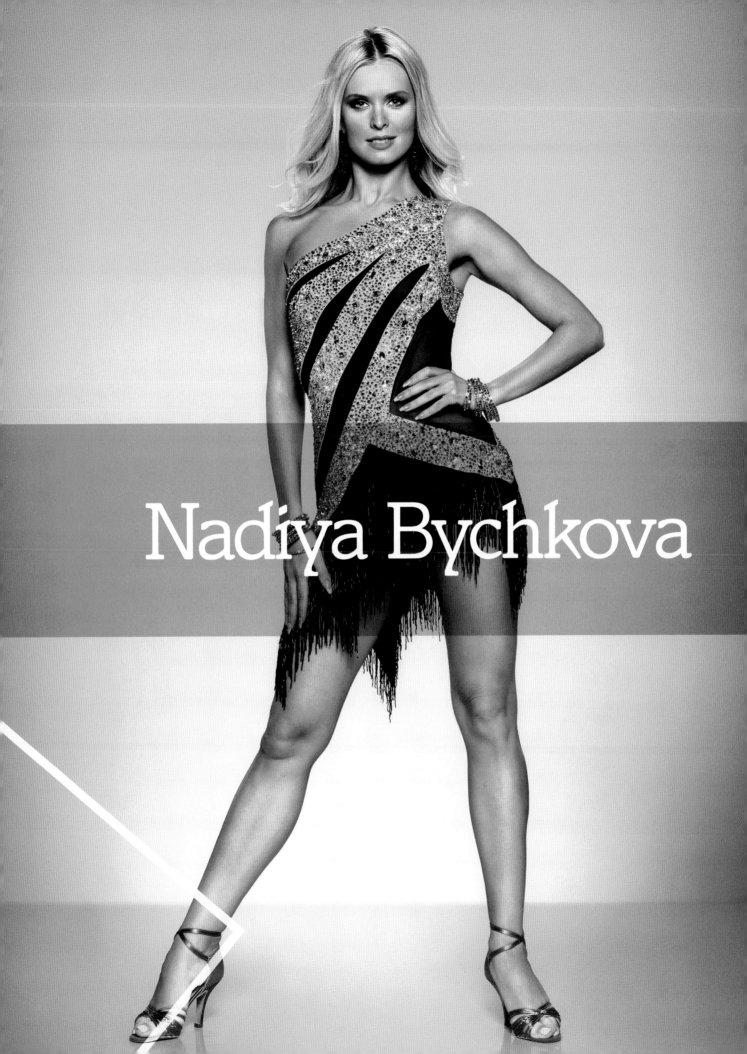

Nadiya Bychkova

The MUSIC MAN

Strictly Come Dancing may be all about the footwork but there would be no show without the music, provided each year by Dave Arch and his wonderful orchestra. The music maestro, with his ever-present headphones and friendly grin, is a familiar sight to viewers from the weekly introduction at the start of the show and this year marks his twelfth series. But Dave still gets a kick out of bringing live music into the nation's living rooms on Saturday nights.

'There are so few live bands like us on television any more,' he says. 'I love the thrill of spending the week writing arrangements and then hearing the band play them, with people dancing and the audience enjoying them. The other thing that is unique to the show is the range of music. You get your standard fare but there are also some obscure styles and I love the variety.'

Dave, a talented pianist, arranger and conductor, has a classical training at the Guildhall School of Music and Drama and joined *Strictly* in series 4. For each series, he writes arrangements for over 200 songs, and that's no mean feat.

'Each song will take, on average, four to five hours. There are some simpler ones that will take three hours and more complicated ones that could take six, but a week of 15 dances and two pro dances means 17 tracks so in the early part of the series, I have a very busy time. The medleys are the most complicated because making all the different songs and tempos blend together is tricky, but it's all part of the challenge.'

For most live shows Dave has an orchestra of 15, comprising of eight brass – three trumpets, two trombones and three saxophones – and a rhythm section of seven, made up of drums, percussion, bass, two guitarists and two keyboard players.

'I sometimes play guitar or percussion so you might see me shaking things or playing something in the background,' he laughs. 'Piano and keyboards are my main instruments but I can play a bit of guitar if I'm behind someone who can do it properly!'

On some occasions, however, extra musicians need to be brought in to complement the core orchestra.

'There are some weeks, such as Movie Week, when we need a bigger sound,' he explains. 'When there's some *Star Wars* or a Rogers and Hammerstein medley, for example, the original track would have 80 or 90 musicians but I have to try and get a bigger sound out of 16 people.

Or there may be a traditional dance like an Argentine tango which needs a bandoneon [a South American accordion], or a violin, so I have to bring in a specialist.'

Although Dave is skilled at putting together any dance number, from a salsa to a foxtrot, he admits he didn't know much about ballroom when he first took up the post.

'I knew what the tempos for a classic waltz, cha-cha and paso doble were, but even now I am guided by the dancers and choreographer Jason Gilkison,' he says. 'Jason can listen to a pop song and say "That's a paso", and I don't always feel that. The tracks are chosen between the dancers and production and I can exaggerate rhythms, especially sambas and salsas, but I am happy to admit I'm not a ballroom specialist.'

But after 12 series on *Strictly*, Dave has learned a lot about ballroom and is always prepared to go the extra mile to make sure the show's music hits all the right notes.

Debbie McGee

Sparkling costumes and glamorous poses are nothing new to Debbie, who found fame as assistant to her magician husband Paul Daniels. But she's hoping to bring her own magic to the dance floor and pull a few tricks out of the bag every Saturday night.

'*Strictly* has all the elements that attracted me to show business,' she reveals. 'I came in because I love pretty dresses and make-up and entertaining audiences.

'As a kid I loved Hollywood movies because I came from a working-class, hard-working background, but my mum and my sister and I would go to the cinema and for that length of time, we would be taken away from everything. That's what *Strictly* does too.'

Debbie grew up in Kingston upon Thames, where her father owned a corner shop, and she showed an interest in dance from a young age. She began dance classes at seven and after living in Iran for a while, she returned to the UK and joined a touring company which laid on entertainment at resorts, finding herself onstage with Paul Daniels for his 1979 Great Yarmouth summer season. When the magician made it on to the nation's screens in the same year, 'the lovely Debbie McGee' was right beside him and, in 1988, the couple wed.

Paul, a former *Strictly* star himself, passed away in 2016, and Debbie says she is keen to show other women in her position that life goes on.

'I've had a few years that have been really tough,' she says. 'I lost my dad and then I lost Paul within 18 months, so the two big men in my life were suddenly gone. But I'm not a person who wants to sit and wallow in sadness and *Strictly* was right for me on every level. It's my mum's favourite show – she records it and watches it and then watches it again in the week – and she's always wanted me to do it so it was something wonderful for my mum and for me too.

'I'm not young. I'm in my late fifties so I'm the oldest and, although I used to dance, I haven't been a dancer since I was 23.

'I just hope there are lots of women out there who are my age, who maybe like me have lost their partners, who realise that you can still have a really good time. Being asked to do the show has been really good for my confidence.'

Debbie is impressed with the standard of her competitors and says they have already bonded as a group.

'Everybody has got it. We are all behind each other. Everybody comes from different backgrounds, we're very diverse, but we all completely gel. We all have chemistry with every single person and there isn't one I don't feel that with. I think because of that we will have a happy time.

'I don't care if I get knocked out first. I have had a ball already and I have met people I will keep in contact with because I really like them.'

Former finalist Giovanni is hoping to bring some magic to the dance floor with his celebrity partner Debbie McGee. But he reveals that the former magician's assistant has a naughty side.

'They call her "the lovely Debbie McGee", but she's quite cheeky and funny,' he says. 'That makes everything much easier because we have so much fun during rehearsals and we get on brilliantly.

'She is a wonderful lady and she's lots of fun. She picks up all the steps really quickly so I'm happy.'

Although she was once a ballet dancer, Debbie hasn't danced for over 35 years.

'The ballet training might help us a little bit but it was a long time ago. But she definitely has rhythm and she loves dancing, so that's fine. We are practising for six hours every day so we are spending a lot of time on the routines and she is very excited about being in the show.'

Born in Sicily. Giovanni wanted to be a dancer from a young age and, at 14, he moved to Bologna to study dance, where he was taught by some of the best teachers in the world. His greatest achievement was winning the Italian Championships in 2012. Giovanni joined *Strictly* in 2015, reaching the final with Georgia May Foote. Last year, he and his partner Laura Whitmore made it to week 7.

'Laura really wanted to learn how to dance, and she was a quick learner,' Giovanni says.

While training for this year, the Italian dancer insists he has not been eyeing up the competition. 'I always focus on my job and think about what I have to do to make my partner look amazing,' he says. 'I concentrate on that and don't look at what the others are doing. My job is to teach my partner to dance.'

With two years under his belt, and a third underway, Giovanni is in no doubt what his favourite moment of each series is.

'I always say the red carpet is my favourite part,' he says. 'Because it's the beginning of the show and when we all get back together with the *Strictly* family. It's the start of a whole new adventure.'

Giovanni Pernice

TOP of the PROPS

From a top hat and cane to swings, spaceships and flying cars, the props bring a little extra magic to each of the *Strictly* dances. In recent years, the increasingly elaborate sets have included a full American diner, a funfair and the *Strictly Express* steam train, but for the talented team behind the design, nothing seems impossible, even at short notice.

'At the start of the series we have a fortnight to create the set,' reveals designer Catherine Land. 'But when the competition is in full swing. It's a very quick turnaround.'

Each week, the pro dancers work with production to come up with the concept for their routine and then Catherine and production designer Patrick Doherty will liaise with producers, costume, hair and make-up to settle on themes and colours. Then Catherine will set to work designing the stage, bearing in mind that every prop and set build has to be brought on and taken off in record time.

'My first consideration is how to make it look amazing,' she admits. 'Then how I can design it so it can be shifted on and off quickly, because if you can't do that it can't go on. There's no point building anything the scenic boys can't set.'

Overseeing the watertight scene-shifting is scenic supervisor Mark Osborne, who has a team of four helpers to perform near miracles between dances. 'We have 90 seconds while the training video runs and, in that time, all the props from the previous dance have to come off and the next ones go on,' he says. 'Everything has to be done as quickly as possible. So it might have to be on wheels, or it might go on a skate,

and it can only be nine feet high.

'Catherine and I will discuss how to make it work so, for example, if she says "They want ten palm trees", I might say, "They can have eight." Because we haven't got the ability to get ten off and get three sets of tables and chairs on at the same time. Then those palm trees would need to be fixed to something, so we might have three on one big skate, because we haven't got time to pick them up and place them individually.'

Smaller items, such as fans, hats, light sabres and *Ghostbuster* guns can be bought in but the bigger 'builds' are custom made.

'The builds are the larger items that set the scene, such as the outside of a theatre, where we'd have a brick wall with sparkly lights all around it, or Frankenstein's table on Halloween week,' explains Catherine. 'Those are all bespoke and I get construction companies to build them off-site. On set, we have one chippy and one painter, plus an extra chippy on Thursdays to help the scenic crew put the builds together for the show.

'I have an assistant to help with the smaller props and we have a wonderful buyer, Bobby Warans, who is the best in the business. If I need something completely random – like a pantomime cow in 24 hours – he will find someone in the country to make one or source one. He always comes up trumps.'

On Thursday, the props begin to arrive at the

Elstree studio and Mark's team will put them together and make any alterations needed to make the switchover easier. The following day, his team get to work honing their set swaps

with split-second precision.

'On Friday we set it up for the first time and do three run-throughs to make sure we can get everything on and off. On Saturday, they get two more rehearsals, then the dress run, which is the only time we get to do it to time before the live show.'

The switch becomes something of a dance in itself, with each of the props boys given their own moves in the routine.

'As soon as we have the running order, we sort out who will move what,' explains Mark. 'The four guys do the majority of the lifting and I organise everything to make sure it happens at the right time. Whatever you do in the rehearsal, you then do on the dress run and on the night, and you don't touch anything else whether there's a problem or not.

'If you do it the first three times and then do something different on the night, someone isn't going to pick up the thing that they should have picked up and that could cost us 15 seconds or more. In telly time, 15 seconds is huge.'

Some sets prove more challenging than others for Catherine and the team.

'One year we had four big water tanks that the pros danced in, for a *Here Comes the Rain/*

THE SECRET OF SPARKLES

With glitter and glamour needed for every set, Catherine has a special way of getting that extra *Strictly* shimmer.

'We have a specialist fabric, encrusted with glitter, which we use to cover everything,' she reveals. 'It's factory-made and comes on a roll, in all sorts of colours, and we can cut that to shape and glue it on to give anything an instant *Strictly* sparkle.

'I love glitter. I can't believe the things I made glittery last year. I even made a twinkling polling station for Jeremy Vine and I never thought I'd do that!'

Umbrella routine,' recalls Catherine. 'It looked amazing but presented a few logistical problems, just coping with a lot of water on set and the amount of water they splashed out. Mark's team were on hand with lots of drying equipment!

'In 2015 we had the train, which was great but again a challenge because it's such a big item. We made a full-sized one for the launch show, which showed up with all the celebs on board, then we used it again for Kevin and Kellie's show dance and we adapted it for the show when we had 90 seconds to set it up. But it worked.'

If things do go wrong at the last minute, all-round handyman Mark can step in. 'You have to be able to build and fix props, because something might snap off or break and suddenly you've got to fix it quickly. So if a table leg falls off you have 30 seconds to screw it back together, and that's part of the excitement. That's why I like it.'

Despite the challenges, Mark, who has worked on the show for over a decade, prides himself on his track record.

'There is no room for error,' he admits. 'The closest shaves have been at Blackpool and Wembley, where the music's starting and we're literally running out of shot just in time but we've never messed up or not got a prop in on time. Touch wood.'

CATHERINE LAND'S TOP FIVE

◆ The *Les Misérables* set for Helen George's paso doble with Aljaž.

'I love Musical Week as you get to go to town on what you can design and it's a break from the glitter! This dance was really dramatic and I hope the set lived up to it.'

◆ The birdcage for the pros' group dance to *Chandelier* by Sia

'We made a beautiful birdcage that Janette danced in and all the others danced around. It was a very stylish routine.'

◆ The art deco lift for Kellie Bright's American smooth with Kevin

'The American smooth is such a sophisticated dance, I wanted to give Kellie and Kevin a really decadent set so I chose art deco as the theme. 'It was influenced by *The Great Gatsby*

which, stylistically, is one of my favourite films.'

◆ The storefront for the pros' group dance to *Thoroughly Modern Millie*

'We made the store called "Goodman's" for Len. It has bags and hat boxes and lots of fancy counters. It was a lovely tribute to him.'

◆ The drums for Ore Oduba and Joanne's show dance to *I Got Rhythm*

'For the Grand Final, Jo and Ore had the huge drum kit that they jumped around during the show dance. It took a lot of planning and rehearsal to get the heights exactly right for Jo and Ore to dance on and they won! Such a lovely couple.'

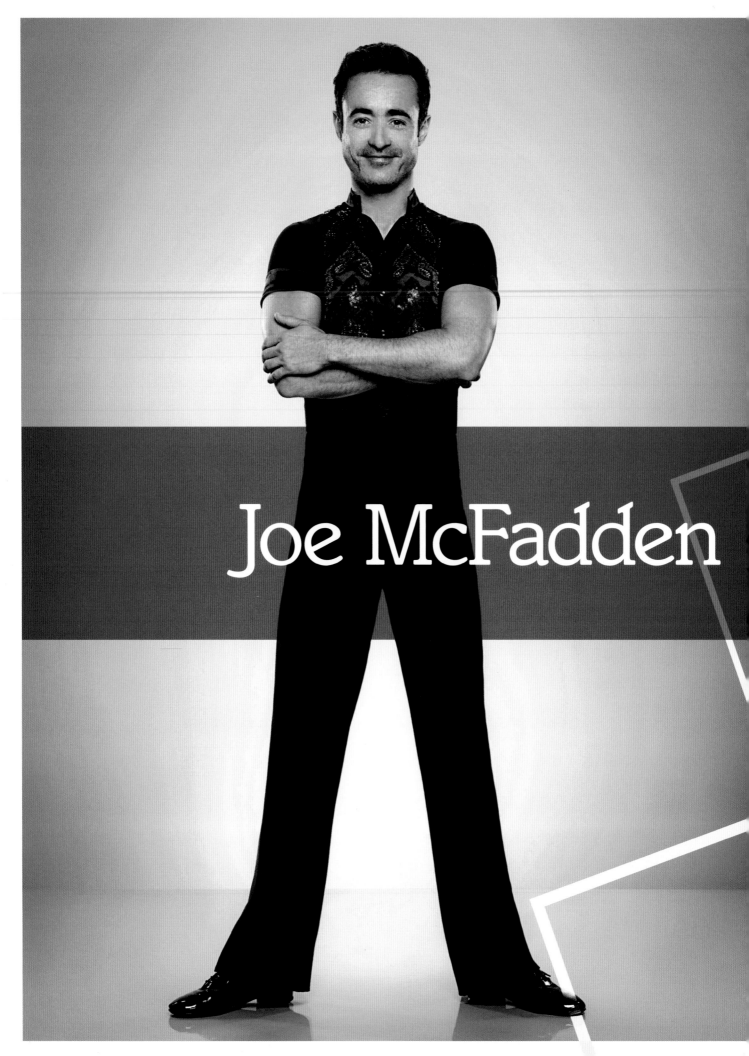

Joe McFadden

Holby City star Joe McFadden is swapping his surgical scrubs for sequins to take to the dance floor – and he couldn't be happier. In fact, the actor, who has played Dr Raf De Lucca in the hospital drama since 2014, is embracing the whole *Strictly* makeover.

'I'm up for the sequins and Lycra, 100 per cent – bring it on,' he laughs. 'The costumes are certainly more sparkly than the scrubs but they are all very comfortable, because they are designed for dancing so they move well and stretch well. As for the spray tan – I'm going full mahogany.'

Joe was born in 1975 in Glasgow, and got his first TV role at the age of 12, when a drama teacher recommended him for a role in detective drama *Taggart*. He went on to star in *Take the High Road* and ITV's long-running *Heartbeat*, in which he played heartthrob copper Joe Mason. He has also starred in *The Crow Road* and numerous films, including *The Trouble With Men and Women* in 2003.

Despite many stints in the theatre, the Glaswegian actor is a novice when it comes to dance but there's one particular routine he can't wait to try.

'I love the Charleston, and I think I should have been born in the 1920s,' he says. 'What I lack in ability I make up for in enthusiasm. I'm that guy at a party who can't stop dancing.'

The Scottish star admits to a few nerves over his live routines, but says his fellow contestants will help see him through.

'Saturday night will be a bit like the opening night of a play, every week,' he says. 'So I imagine it will be terrifying. Every day there's a new thing to take on, like a rehearsal or a costume fitting, but we're all in it together and we're all supporting each other.'

Joe is not the only *Holby* doctor to be dancing his way through Saturday night as former co-star Chizzy Akudolu, who left the show earlier this year, is also competing. But Joe insists there's no rivalry between the two.

'We're not going head to head, we're flying the flag together, and it's lovely to have a friendly, familiar face here,' he explains. 'We've got each other's backs.'

While he is looking forward to throwing himself into training, the Scottish star won't be neglecting his medical duties, and will be filming both shows at the Elstree studios throughout the *Strictly* run.

'I have some big storylines coming up in *Holby* and I will be filming at the same time, but the great thing is that, as we film in the same place, we can fit rehearsals in between scenes. People have done it in the past. Jake Wood, who I know had big storylines in *EastEnders* while he was on the show, had a fantastic time doing it, and so did Kellie Bright, so it is doable – with a lot of caffeine.'

Last year marked Katya's debut on the *Strictly* dance floor but her routines, with partner Ed Balls, are already the stuff of legend. The former politician's *Mask*-themed samba and *Gangnam Style* salsa made him a fan favourite and saw him dancing his way through to week 10.

'We had a ball,' says Katya. 'As well as working hard, we had so much fun. I'm so happy that it made people smile.'

World Latin Champion Katya was born in St Petersburg, Russia and started dancing at the age of six, training in gymnastics as well as ballroom and Latin. In 2008, Katya formed a partnership with Neil Jones, and together they went on to win the World Amateur Latin Championships three times, before turning professional, and getting married, in 2013. Two years later, they became the World Professional Latin Showdance Champions and are four times undefeated British National Professional Champions.

After her success with Ed, Katya is looking forward to dancing with *Holby City* star Joe McFadden and says her *Strictly* debut has been the perfect grounding for the new challenge.

'My first year was wonderful,' she says. 'Considering I didn't know all the pros, we soon became one big group and everybody is so nice. We became massive friends. And after getting Ed, and the great run we had together, I don't think it could have gone any better. To make a big statement coming in was so good for me so I'm really excited for this year, to be able to show more of what I can do, with new choreography and new dancing.'

Joe, she says, is showing 'lots of promise' despite being thrown in the deep end with an energetic jive for his first dance.

'The jive needs so much energy from beginning to end and the routine is so fast that if you lose one bit, it's all out, so you need a lot of concentration,' says Katya. 'In the first few days, doing the jive for eight hours a day, Joe was up for new legs. But each day brings so much improvement and you build it up so he got used the moves and used to the energy. He says he's dancing while he's washing the dishes at home, so he uses every spare moment.'

Katya Jones

Bruno Tonioli

Ebullient Italian Bruno Tonioli is looking forward to welcoming new judge Shirley Ballas, who he already counts as a friend.

'I know Shirley very well, and she will be great on the judging panel,' says Bruno. 'When I was in America we lived in the same apartment block. She trained Derek and Julianne Hough, and other dancers on *Dancing with the Stars*, and she is an incredibly respected dance coach. I don't think you could find anybody more qualified.'

As always, Bruno is excited about the 2017 line-up, but he's not risking any predictions.

'With *Strictly* you can never tell what's going to happen,' he says. 'Look at last year! You think you can predict a winner but it all turns upside down by the end of the series. Having done it for so many years I try and keep my mind open. But they look good on paper.'

Is there anyone you have your eye on already?

I'm looking forward to seeing Jonnie Peacock, as he will be very competitive. There is an element of determination and the will to succeed that brings a high level of competition to the series.

Will previous dance experience help the singers, such as Aston and Mollie?

We always have people with some dance experience – last year it was Danny Mac and Louise Redknapp – but it actually makes little difference to the final result. People coming from behind are often the ones that the public get really involved with. Ore had no dance experience but he peaked at the right time.

Will Shirley be a tough judge?

Shirley is a Northerner and has a feisty sense of humour. She is from the generation who took the evolution of ballroom to a much more athletic level so it became more spectacular and demanding. She knows how to push people physically and judging by her teaching, I don't think Shirley will let the contestants get away with anything!

What did you think of last year's final?

What a brilliant show. Right up to the show dance, it could have gone any of three ways. Joanne and Ore played it very well. They were creative in their numbers. A show like *Strictly* is like a tennis match – you have to play the big points when they matter.

What are your favourite memories of Bruce Forsyth?

I always had such a laugh with Bruce. I worked with him as a dancer back in the day, and he was always a generous performer to share the stage with. Because of where I sat on the *Strictly* panel, we always exchanged a few words as he came in and out and he had a sixth sense about what worked. If you were on to a good thing he let you run with it, and would make it funnier. I miss him, but as he said himself, he wouldn't want us to moan and groan because he would want us to laugh and a have a celebration.

Mollie King

Singer Mollie is hoping to bring some sparkle to your Saturdays when she takes to the dance floor and says the more glitz and glamour the better.

'I feel like I'm living in a glitter dream at the moment,' she says. 'I'm really looking forward to genuinely learning to dance with my partner. Of course, performing every Saturday night is going to be so exciting. I love the costumes and I love a cheeky spray tan.'

Mollie was born in London in 1987, and brought up in Kingston upon Thames. As a child she was a champion skier, joining the British Children's Ski Team at 11 and winning a scholarship to the British Ski Academy. She raced for Great Britain and later went on to ski for the British Alpine squad before shelving a career in the sport to pursue her dream of becoming a singer.

In signing up for *Strictly*, the singer follows her Saturdays bandmate Frankie Bridge, who was runner up in the 2014 final.

'I've wanted to do it ever since I saw Frankie do it, so I can't believe I am here,' she says. 'Frankie just said to enjoy every minute and she said it would go by so quickly. So I need to lap it up, enjoy it as much as possible, and really throw myself into it and rehearse my socks off.'

Although pop fans have seen Mollie performing live on numerous tours, she is adamant that dancing has never been her strength. Just ask her mum.

'I've performed with The Saturdays, but we never really did full-on dance routines, it was more just poses or moving around the stage,' she said. 'I've never actually done anything like this. I went to a ballet class when I was about three and they told my mum that she was wasting her money taking me there because I had no grace at all, so my mum took me out and put me in football class instead. I'm hoping I'll be a bit more graceful now.'

Her mum is over the moon to see her girl finally make it on to the dance floor.

'My family are so excited I had to warn them not to tell anyone before it was announced,' she reveals. 'My mum, particularly, was sworn to secrecy. Even after it was announced she said, "Don't worry, I haven't told anyone." I said, "Mum, you can tell people now." They are beyond excited and I think they want to get the neighbours round and just about everyone they've ever met.'

Mollie admits to being very competitive and adds, 'Everyone here would love to lift up the glitter ball. Who wouldn't? But I just want to stay in as long as I can and learn a few dances so I can pull them out at friends' weddings.'

This year, AJ will be spending his Saturdays on the dance floor with singer Mollie King and he's raring to go.

'Until Tess says who I am dancing with I am so nervous, but as soon as she said it was Mollie my head was full of ideas and I just wanted to get started straight away.

'Training is a ball. We are laughing and joking the whole time. We're training eight hours a day and it just flies by, so I couldn't be happier to get Mollie.'

The couple were thrown in at the deep end in week 1, with an energetic jive to the aptly titled *Good Golly Miss Molly*, and AJ admits it came as a bit of a shock to his new pupil.

'It was a bit of a wake-up call for Mollie, realising that the first dance will make you sweat every single day, because we will be doing it again and again, but it shows the reality of the hard training, which is good.'

While she has appeared in music videos throughout her pop career, Mollie is an absolute beginner in the dance class.

'She's never done any dance training before and never done theatre or drama school. I am teaching her from scratch, which in a way is good because there are no bad habits.

'Mollie has a great personality and when she feels comfortable with the steps, which is starting to happen, I can see her personality coming out a bit more and I can't wait to see it happen on the live shows.'

Born in Stoke-on Trent, AJ learned to dance at his parents' dance school, where he was paired with his professional dance partner Chloe Hewitt. In 2015, the talented twosome won the British Open Youth Latin Champions and also became European Youth Latin Champions. Together they have set records by becoming the National Youth Latin Champions for three years in a row from 2012 to 2014.

In his first outing on the show last year he was partnered with gymnast Claudia Fragapane and the couple made the semi-finals.

'Claudia was very good. She and Mollie have two completely different personalities,' says AJ. 'Claudia was very focused and driven, being an Olympian. With Mollie, it feels quite relaxed on camera, and we can do different dance styles.'

AJ, the youngest of the male dancers, says he is more confident going into his second year on *Strictly*.

'I'm feeling very positive this year,' he says. 'I know the system, I know what to expect. I know the order of everything, what happens on Halloween week, Blackpool week, and how crazy it can get on a Saturday, and on the Friday rehearsals with the band calls and dress runs. Last year, I was saying to Claudia, "It's new for both of us, so we're going to experience this together." This year, I'm prepared and I can explain it to Mollie.'

AJ Pritchard

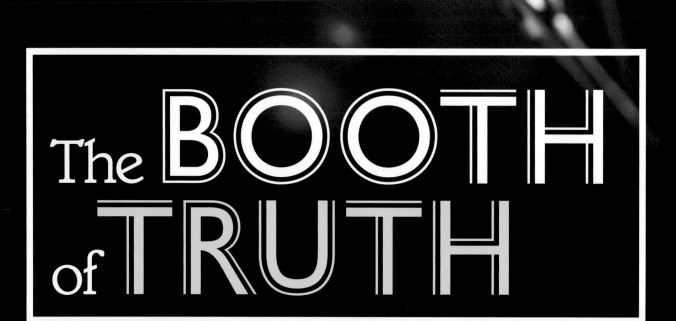

The BOOTH of TRUTH

Taking a leaf out of the It Takes Two book, we fired some random questions at the *Strictly* dancers – and here's what they had to say.

Do you have any superstitions?

Chloe: 'Ever since I was a young girl I've always saluted a magpie for good luck. My nan got me into that, now I can't stop doing it.'

Aljaž: 'Before a dance, I check my zipper about a million times. I know I did it about 20 seconds ago but I always have to check again.'

Oti: 'Collecting hairbands on my arm. On week one I start with no hairbands and then get one every week and I don't take them off. Every week I add different colours, so I get into trouble with the wardrobe team because they are the wrong colour for the dresses.'

Who's the biggest joker in the pack?

Giovanni: 'Neil Jones. He tells jokes that sometimes are funny and sometimes are not, so we pretend to laugh. He also plays pranks, like putting water in shoes.'

Oti: 'Neil Jones. One joke a week is great, but he is joking every second.'

Aljaž: 'Between Neil Jones and Anton. Anton finds a new joke every day. With him there is never a dull moment in rehearsals.'

(For the record, every dancer named Mr Jones, so we find him guilty as charged.)

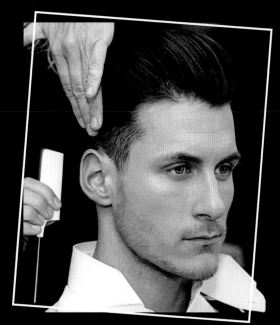

Gorka always makes sure he looks his best

Never a dull moment backstage with Strictly's resident joker Neil

Who is the vainest?

Janette: 'Gorka.'

Aljaž: 'Judging from the amount of selfies, AJ. He's the only person I know where the camera on the front of the phone matters more than the one on the back.'

Oti: 'Selfies, mirrors, checking himself out – that's AJ.'

Chloe: 'That would have to be my partner AJ. I don't think he's ever walked past a piece of reflective material without checking himself out. The Selfie King!'

Who would you like to cook you dinner?

Chloe: 'Karen loves to cook up a great dinner so she would be a great person to dine with.'

Janette: 'Aljaž. Neither of us are good cooks but that's why it's okay, because if he cooks for me I won't judge.'

What's your most annoying habit?

Janette: 'A weird one, but I have banana with everything. Literally, banana with spaghetti, banana with chicken and rice, banana with noodles. It comes from my Cuban upbringing when we had fried plantain on the side with everything.'

Giovanni: 'Biting my nails. Horrid.'

Karen: 'I love to chew gum while I'm dancing.'

Aljaž: 'Janette. It would be more special because it rarely happens!'

AJ: 'Main course, I think Pasha would be a fantastic cook, he always watches what he eats. Then dessert – I love Gorka's Pancakes. Yes, they're protein, but great with ice cream.'

Giovanni: 'My best friends, Aljaž and Kevin – we're The Three Musketeers. It's always good to chat and have a laugh with them.'

The Three Musketeers: Kevin, Aljaž and Giovanni

Oti: 'Anton. I don't know if he can cook but he's a gentleman so I feel like he would have a nice table and candle and roses and some ballroom classical music. Or Brendan, who is like a big brother to me.'

What is your favourite meal?

Janette: 'My grandma's home-cooked Cuban meal is the best. It's fried plantains, rice and black beans with chicken or steak. I miss it so much.'

Aljaž: 'My mum's spaghetti or my dad's Ćevapčići. It's a minced meat, like a skinless sausage, that you grill outside.'

Giovanni: 'Pasta with tuna. I love tuna. I can't cook so I buy the sauce and just open it and throw it on the pasta.'

Karen: 'Skirt steak with mashed sweet potato and a side of spinach salad with tomatoes and avocado.'

AJ: 'I do love a perfectly cooked steak. Heaven. Rare. For dessert, I do absolutely love chocolate, chocolate cake or just anything covered in chocolate, or sticky toffee pudding or honeycomb ice cream or CHOCOLATE brownie with honeycomb ice cream. You get the picture.'

Chloe: 'My mum's roast dinner. Delicious'.

Oti: 'Ribs and fries with coleslaw and a good cocktail. That is so me.'

Who has the best sense of style?

Giovanni: 'Katya. She designs her own dresses and tells us what to wear.'

Chloe: 'I love Katya's sense of style. She is so creative and adventurous. I've already mentioned I want her to be my personal stylist.'

Style queen Katya

Katya: 'Sorry to say, it's me.'

Aljaž: 'Anton always looks immaculate and so does Pasha but I always love the Italian style of Giovanni. You can always pick him out in a crowd.'

AJ: 'If we are talking suited and booted, then Anton is on it... always a perfect combination and a different tie, smart on every occasion, even in training. 'Then you have Katya. She will always dare to be different and I love her for it.'

Do you have a pet?

Karen: 'Kevin and I adopted our dog Betty from Bosnia. She was found living rough on the streets but now has a for ever home with us. She is kind, loving, loves watching squirrels and a good belly tickle.'

Oti: 'A little doggie called Joey. But he's in South Africa and causes my mum stress because she rings me and says, "Your dog is eating my couches and my pillows and my cabbages." But he's so sweet'

Katya: 'CRUMBLE!!! She's the cutest little dog. She's is chihuahua/shih-tzu/toy poodle mix. She's very lazy and she loves Neil.'

Chloe: 'I have a cat. He's very lazy. The kind of animal that every human would want to be because all he does is eat and sleep. I also have a six-month-old German spitz puppy. A complete ray of sunshine. Always happy and full of energy.'

What do you have for breakfast?

Oti: 'Baked beans with pepper and tabasco, bread and avocado. With ginger and apple juice.'

Giovanni: 'Croissant and espresso.'

Karen: 'Pancakes with bacon and a big cup of coffee.'

Katya: 'Yogurt with granola and berries.'

Chloe: 'A boiled egg or an omelette and, of course, a coffee. Can't start my day without one.'

What's the last thing you do before hitting the *Strictly* floor?

Janette: 'I give my partner a high five, look him in the eyes and say "We've got this. We can do it", and give them a last boost of confidence. By the time that moment comes, they've put in all the effort and time and they have to just enjoy it.'

AJ: 'I literally scream at myself in a corner to hype myself up and get into the zone, get the adrenalin pumping.'

Karen: 'Have a piece of chocolate. It makes me extra happy and a little hyper.'

Katya: 'Breathe.'

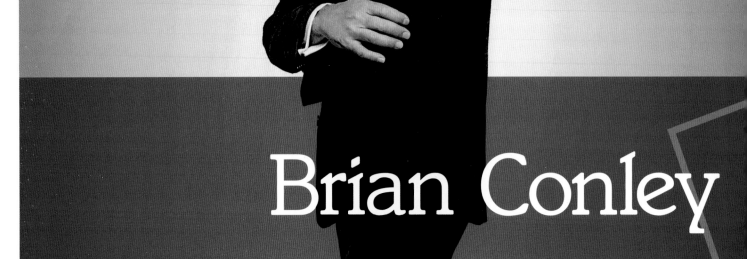

Brian Conley

For comedian Brian, *Strictly Come Dancing* really is a family affair. Not only does his brother Alan Conley work behind the scenes on the show, but one of his two daughters is such a fan it made it impossible for him to pass on the challenge.

'My daughter Lucy said, "Dad, if you love me, you'd do *Strictly*," so that's what happened,' he reveals. 'That's one of the many reasons I'm here and the whole family are really looking forward to it.

'My brother Al is the floor manager and has been there since the second series. He's always told me, "You should do it."'

Born in Paddington in 1961, Brian grew up wanting to be an entertainer and got a job as a Pontins blue coat in his teens. He was talent-spotted at 19 while working with a touring comedy group in pubs and clubs, and became a warm-up man for big TV acts, including The Krankies and Kenny Everett, before being awarded comedy slots on ITV variety shows and eventually his own primetime show, *Brian Conley: This Way Up*. In the 1990s, the comic fronted *The Brian Conley Show*, a variety programme, as well as starring in sitcom *Time After Time* and the comedy drama *The Grimleys*.

More recently, he appeared in the reality show *I'm a Celebrity* but had to leave early on medical grounds.

Fans will remember 'Dangerous Brian', but the comedian will be playing it straight on the dance floor.

'I'll leave Dangerous Brian in the dressing room because I think they'll say, "Brian, stop playing to the gallery, this is all about dancing," and that's why I'm here. On the night, I'll be focused.'

Brian is a huge fan of *Strictly* and is thrilled to be taking to the floor.

'It's the biggest show on television and it's very much been a part of my family and my life for a long time,' he explains. 'I've always loved it. I loved Bruce Forsyth and the light-entertainment side of it, and it's such a happy show, and that's what makes it so successful. It's a wonderful bit of escapism, so it's a wonderful honour to be here.'

The cheeky chappy promises he won't be giving any lip to the judges for one simple reason.

'I don't think I will banter with them and you know why? Because I'll be too out of breath!' He laughs. 'Whenever you see someone at the end of the dance they are gasping for breath, so I'm thinking of getting an oxygen mask.'

Comedian Brian Conley is in capable hands as he takes to the *Strictly* dance floor, because his partner, new girl Amy, is the current British National Champion and one of the highest-ranking ballroom and Latin American dancers in the UK. The Welsh dancer started learning at an early age, after winning her first accolade on a family holiday.

'I was eight years old and I'd been on holiday to a campsite in Cornwall,' she reveals. 'There was a disco-dancing competition at the clubhouse, which I won. When we went home I begged my mum to take me to dancing, so the following Saturday she took me to a dance class and I started learning Latin and ballroom.'

Amy danced in a formation team for several years and took up ballet and contemporary dance at 14. At 16, she began competing and has since racked up four British National finals with partner Ben Jones, taking the title in 2016, as well as competing in the semi-finals of the World Championships and coming fourth in the Ultimate World Cup challenge last year.

Amy admits to shedding a few tears of joy when she was chosen for the new series of *Strictly*.

'I was ecstatic,' she recalls. 'I started crying on the phone. I rang my dad and he was in his work van, and he burst into tears as well.

'I've watched *Strictly* since I was 11 years old and it's always been one of my wildest dreams to dance on the show. It's a fantastic show. It has that fairy-tale quality, so everybody warms to it.'

Amy, from Caerphilly, is thrilled to be paired with Brian and, while the pair may be laughing their way through rehearsals, they are serious about their routines.

'I was super excited to be partnered with Brian,' she says. 'I had a feeling anyway, because when we first met the celebrities, I got talking to Brian and I couldn't stop laughing, so I think the producers could see that we had a good rapport and a good chemistry. We're having lots of fun but he is willing to work hard, which is really important and we are going to put in as many hours as we can.'

Amy, whose favourite dance is the rumba, is happy with the progress of her pupil so far.

'He's not looking bad at all. He seems to be equally good at both ballroom and Latin but he definitely prefers the faster dances to the slower ones.'

One of three new professionals on the show, Amy says she has been welcomed into the fold by the other dancers but admits to a few nerves ahead of the series.

'I am nervous but I think that's good,' she admits. 'My dance teacher used to say that the minute you are not nervous, it's time to hang up your dance shoes because it means you don't care. Nerves show you are passionate about it.

'Brian and I are both working really hard to create a great routine. I just want to enjoy it and show everybody the hours of training we've put in.'

Amy Dowden

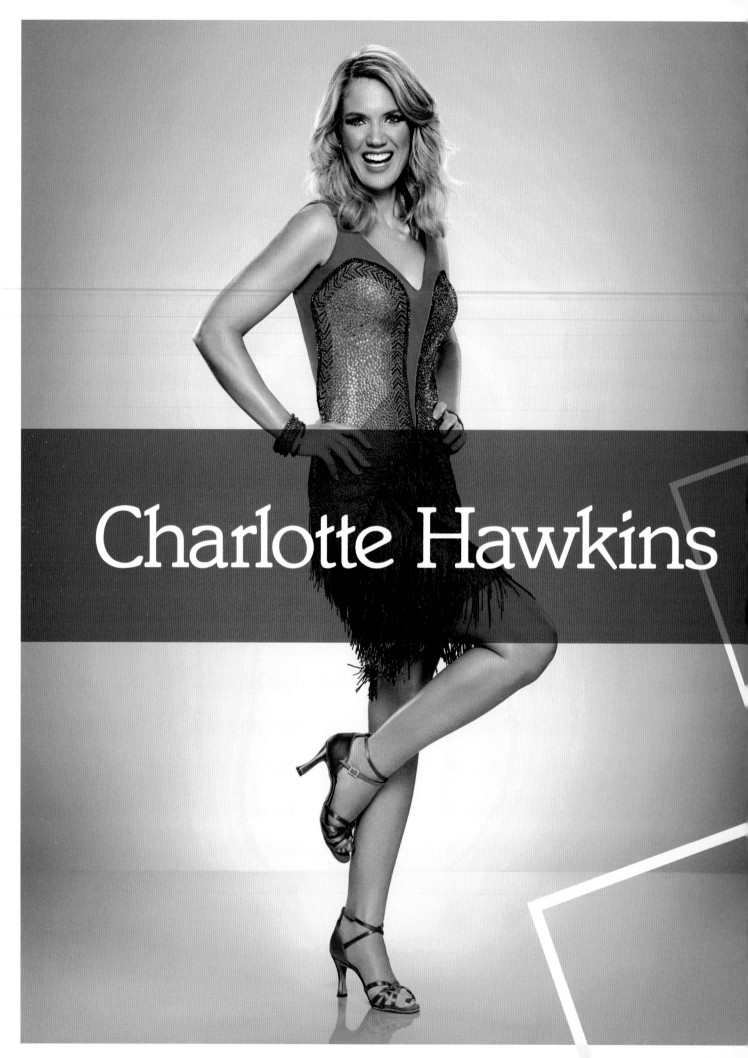

Charlotte Hawkins

After years of presenting the news on the small screen, Charlotte was able to announce her own signing to *Strictly* in her morning news bulletin, before taking to the floor with former contestant Richard Arnold.

'Richard and I did a little twirl around the studio and I managed not to trip over, which was quite an achievement,' she laughs. 'I was really pleased to be able to break my own news on *Good Morning Britain* and it's nice that Richard and Susanna Reid have been through it before so they can give me an idea of what to expect.'

News anchor Susanna, who reached the final with Kevin Clifton in series 11, sent Charlotte a supportive message as soon as she heard.

'She said, "just have a ball", and said that even though it is scary and intimidating dancing in front of all those people, don't forget to really enjoy it, throw yourself into it and make the most of the experience,' says Charlotte. 'I'm going to be asking her for her top tips and she'll also be coming along to support me.'

Charlotte studied English Literature at Manchester University before taking a post-graduate course in broadcast journalism and landing a job as a reporter at LBC. After moving into local television, and hosting *Meridian Tonight* in the South-East, she went on to a high profile role at *Sky News*. In 2014, she joined the team at *Good Morning Britain*.

As well as juggling the day job with her training, Charlotte is mum to two-year-old Ella Rose, and plans to get her involved.

'I'm going to have to be organised about it because I am going to be doing *Good Morning Britain*, then training all day, and I obviously want to make sure I spend a decent amount of time with my daughter,' she admits.

'But the nice thing is she loves dancing and watching *Strictly* so I will do extra training with her when I get home, and we can dance round together in the lounge.'

The broadcaster reveals she is enjoying the 'little magical, sparkly, glittery world' before the hard work begins.

'As much as we're loving it, this is the fun bit,' she says. 'Then comes the real hard-core training, day after day, then we're standing backstage saying, "we've got to go and dance in front of millions of people". That might be the scary side of our magical bubble.'

But she confesses the hardest thing could be keeping a straight face during the sexy or romantic dances.

'I'm a little worried because when you dance really close to someone it's a bit like being a 15-year-old again,' she laughs. 'We did a bit of dancing, where all the guys had to go round from girl to girl because they were trying to work out who was going to go well together. But I couldn't keep a straight face." I have to get over that but I assume that the more I dance, the easier that will get.'

Strictly original Brendan was the first professional ever to lift the hallowed glitter ball, with newsreader Natasha Kaplinsky. This year he's back with another TV journalist, Charlotte Hawkins, and says he 'can't wait to get started'.

The *Good Morning Britain* star has even come up with a catchy name for the duo – Team Charcole – which means they will soon be burning up the dance floor.

Brendan was born in Christchurch, New Zealand and started dancing at the age of six, following in the footsteps of his brother Scott and sister Vanessa, who have both been champions on *Dancing with the Stars* in their native country. Brendan moved to the UK at the age of 18, working as a roofer and a builder while pursuing his dance career. Brendan and his then partner Camilla Dallerup became the New Zealand and Asian Open Professional Champions and were semi-finalists at the International, UK Open, British Open and World Championships.

After winning the first ever series of *Strictly Come Dancing* in 2004, Brendan has reached the Grand Final on two more occasions, with Lisa Snowdon, in series 6, and Sophie Ellis Bextor in series 11.

'With Lisa we got a perfect score in the final, which was pretty epic,' he says. 'And I'm really proud of my series with Sophie.'

Brendan's other partners have included Jo Wood, Michelle Williams, Lulu, Claire King, Fiona Phillips and Kirsty Gallacher. Last year he danced with American singer, Anastacia, and the couple were eliminated in week 6.

Throughout his *Strictly* career, Brendan has produced many unforgettable dances with his partners, and he and Lisa remain the only couple, apart from Caroline Flack and Pasha Kovalev, to have achieved a perfect score for the cha-cha.

This year Brendan's been impressed by partner Charlotte's approach to training. 'I'm chuffed with the whole attitude,' he says. 'She's really trying to get all the elements.' He's hoping this hard-working attitude will take them all the way to the final.

Brendan Cole

Word Search

Are you eagle-eyed as well as fleet of foot? Waltz around our word search and see how many you can spot.

T	H	J	K	F	N	S	H	L	F	J	N	F	A	G
P	A	S	O	D	O	B	L	E	G	I	A	F	B	N
G	X	M	Z	T	L	A	G	I	Y	H	U	E	M	V
N	E	T	E	N	P	G	V	N	C	Y	H	B	J	A
Y	T	N	Q	R	M	W	D	A	N	C	E	O	F	F
R	H	I	D	P	I	R	H	B	W	F	H	R	V	O
E	G	T	G	P	H	C	M	X	U	N	R	I	N	X
B	I	A	S	C	R	Y	A	B	A	D	Y	U	F	T
Z	T	L	A	W	E	S	E	N	N	E	I	V	S	R
S	L	S	C	A	V	U	G	E	S	J	R	N	O	O
P	L	E	B	A	L	L	R	O	O	M	O	P	G	T
A	A	M	A	Z	B	R	O	O	M	H	O	I	N	C
J	U	I	H	A	W	M	V	A	G	L	K	O	A	G
R	U	H	F	J	D	Q	A	E	K	Q	A	R	T	K
H	D	C	E	V	I	J	E	S	T	Z	H	N	G	H

American smooth
Ballroom
Cha-cha

Dance off
Foxtrot
Jive

Latin
Paso doble
Rumba

Tango
Viennese waltz

Strictly Quiz

Are you in step with *Strictly*? Try our quiz to find out if you glide with ease or stumble over *Strictly* trivia.

1 Which dance was added in series 7 and is still danced in the main show?

2 Name the three actors who have been crowned *Strictly* champions.

3 Which song did last year's champions Ore Oduba and Joanne Clifton perform the tango to for their first ever dance on *Strictly*?

4 Who is the only professional to have won the main series trophy twice?

5 Which two professionals have been on the show the longest?

6 Which professional has danced in the most finals?

7 How long is the average *Strictly* routine?

8 What song did Louis Smith and Flavia Cacace perform to for their winning show dance in series 10?

9 Which American superstar guest judged in series 12?

10 Who was the first celebrity partner for Aljaž Skorjanec?

11 Which couple scored two perfect 40s in the 2015 final?

12 Which two judges have also sat on the panel of the US show *Dancing with the Stars*?

13 Which celebrity was fired from a cannon at Wembley in 2011?

The youngest of the professional dancers, Chloe joined the cast last year, along with professional dance partner AJ Pritchard. As an avid fan, who took up dancing after watching the first series when she was eight, working on *Strictly* was a dream come true.

'My first year was so much fun and it was amazing to be a part of a show that I'd watched for so many years,' she says. 'It was really interesting to see how it all works backstage and how they put this wonderful show together.'

Despite her excitement, Chloe admits to some nerves on her first day – but she says the other professionals welcomed her with open arms.

'I remember my first group rehearsal. I was petrified because all the others knew each other, and AJ and I knew nobody. I was nervous, wondering if they were going to take to us, because you have the likes of Anton and Brendan who have been there since day one, and we were the new kids on the block. But they took us in as if we had been there for years and that was incredible because it's a working environment and you want to feel good and feel part of it, and they made sure that we did.'

The Chester-born dancer teamed up with AJ after attending the dance school run by his parents. In 2015, they became British Open Youth Latin Champions and European Youth Latin Champions and had previously broken a record by becoming National Youth Latin Champions for three years in a row, from 2012–14.

Although she didn't have a celebrity in the main series, Chloe performed in all the group dances as well as becoming a regular on *It Takes Two*, where the tables were turned and she found herself learning new dance disciplines.

'I learned belly dancing and hip hop and it put me out of my comfort zone but I really enjoyed it,' she says. 'I went into it not knowing what to expect, so I felt like a celebrity would feel on *Strictly*. But you have to throw yourself into it and forget about whether it's embarrassing or scary. Belly dancing was so hard. They make it look so effortless, so I was like, "OK, I've got this", but I really hadn't.'

The Christmas special saw Chloe quickstepping with her first celebrity partner, series 5 finalist Gethin Jones, and she also travelled the country in the live tour.

'Being part of the Christmas special is magical, because it really got us in the festive mood,' she says. 'Gethin is an amazing guy and it was a bonus that he had already danced before. We had so much fun.

'The tour was an amazing experience. Going to these huge arenas and seeing them packed with people who adore the show was overwhelming. I never thought in my wildest dreams I would ever perform at the O2 arena so that was something else!'

This year Chloe will be popping up more often on *It Takes Two*, and will also be in all the group dances on the live shows.

'I'm looking forward to all the group dances, which are going to be incredible this year,' she says. 'I cannot wait to get involved in all of those.'

Chloe Hewitt

Strictly pro Neil is looking forward to another stellar series, after joining the show last year.

Neil was born in a British Army Camp in Munster, Germany, and started dancing at a local ballet school at the age of three. He specialised in ballroom and Latin and also trained in tap, modern and ballet. In 2008, he met Katya at the British Open Championships in Blackpool and the pair teamed up, becoming the undefeated four-time British National Champions and the three-time winners of the World Amateur Latin Championships. They married in 2013, and two years later were crowned World Professional Latin Showdance Champions.

As part of the *Strictly* pro team, Neil performs in all the group dances, as well as lending his expertise to Choreography Corner on *It Takes Two*, along with Chloe Hewitt.

'I had a lot of fun moments on *It Takes Two*,' he says. 'On one show Katya and I went on to hear our results for the pro challenge – when we tried to do as many jive kicks and flicks as possible in 30 seconds – and I thought I'd won because they came back with a figure of 104, double everybody's score. I did a celebration dance and then Zoe Ball said, "All 104 were disqualified" – so I came bottom. I'm never going to live that down.

'I also learnt some bhangra and Cossack dancing which was an experience. I got the bhangra quite quickly but I remember looking at the Cossack dancers and thinking I'm a dancer – how hard can it be? It was so hard! I looked at them all after that with new respect. The flexibility and the strength in their legs is amazing.'

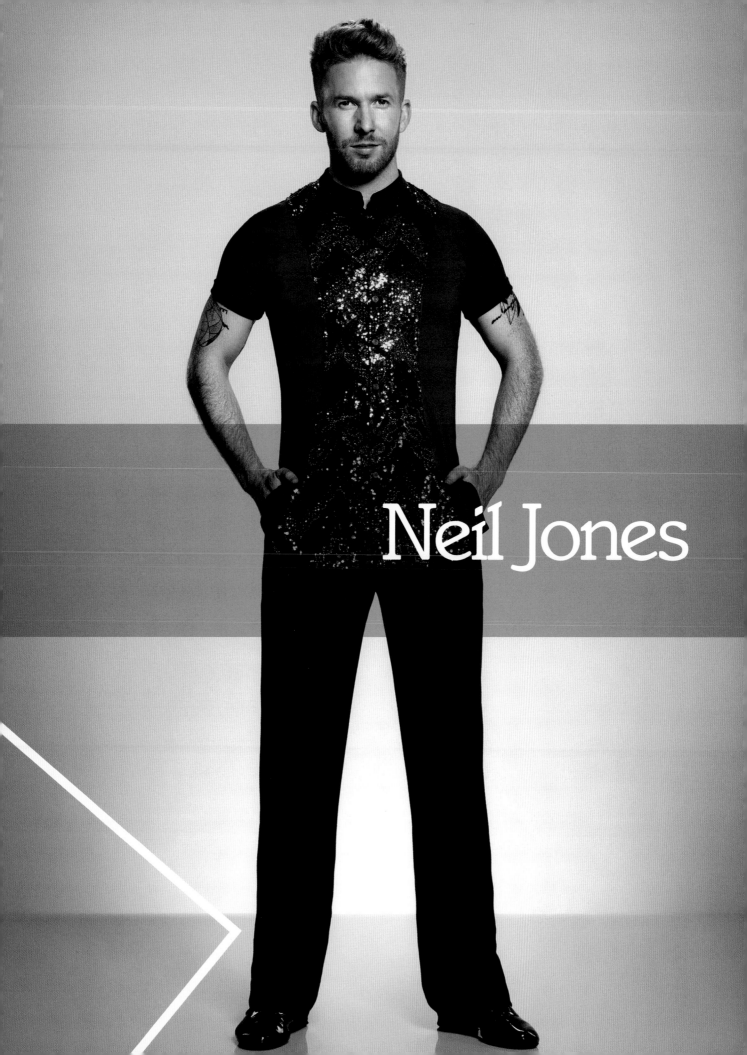

Neil Jones

Photograph p28 © Metheven Bond
Photographs pp. 7, 17, 20, 23, 30, 33, 35, 36, 39, 44, 47, 49, 54, 57, 60,
63, 68, 71, 73, 74, 77, 82, 85, 86, 89, 92, 95, 100, 103, 105, 106, 109,
114, 117, 118, 121, 125, 127 © BBC/Ray Burmiston
Photographs pp. 9–11, 13–15, 40, 43, 51–53, 64–65, 79–81, 91, 97–99
© BBC/Guy Levy
All other photographs © BBC

10 9 8 7 6 5 4 3 2 1

BBC Books, an imprint of Ebury Publishing
20 Vauxhall Bridge Road, London SW1V 2SA

BBC Books is part of the Penguin Random House group of companies
whose addresses can be found at global.penguinrandomhouse.com

Penguin
Random House
UK

The BBC would like to thank Tessa Beckett, Selena Harvey, Jack Gledhill,
Richard Curwen, Louise Rainbow, Victoria Dalton and Kate Lawson.

This book is published to accompany the television series entitled
Strictly Come Dancing first broadcast on BBC One in 2017.

Executive producer: Louise Rainbow
Series director: Nikki Parsons
Series producer: Robin Lee-Perrella
Series editor: Sarah James

First published by BBC Books in 2017

www.penguin.co.uk

A CIP catalogue record for this book is available from the British Library

ISBN 9781785942068

Printed and bound in Italy by Rotolito Lombarda SpA

Penguin Random House is committed to a sustainable future for our
business, our readers and our planet. This book is made from Forest
Stewardship Council® certified paper.

MIX
Paper from
responsible sources
FSC® C018179